Drama to Inspire

a London Drama Guide to excellent practice
in drama for young people

Drama to Inspire
a London Drama Guide to excellent practice in drama for young people

edited by John Coventon
Foreword by Cecily O'Neill

Trentham Books
Stoke on Trent, UK and Sterling, USA

WORKING TOGETHER

Speech Bubbles – Adam Annand • 139
*London Bubble and educational psychologists working
with Key Stage 1 pupils needing support*

Quicksilver Theatre; Primary Voices – Carey English • 153
From child script idea to professional performance

Creative Learning in the ATG – Julia Potts and John Coventon • 169
*How commercial theatre supports learning in
schools and the community*

About London Drama – Chris Lawrence • 179
*The professional organisation for teachers and others,
past, present and future*

THE LAST WORD

Article 31 – UN Convention of the Rights of the Child • 187

The Contributors • 189

Index • 193

Foreword

Cecily O'Neill

In 1916 John Dewey insisted that model lesson plans and recipes had nothing to do with education. Instead of depending on such a sterile and limited pedagogy, he argued, it is the reconstruction and articulation of experience that are at the core of education. The title of this book, *Drama to Inspire*, indicates that the kind of reductive approaches condemned by Dewey have no place between its covers.

Drama teaching is a vocation that can be both professionally and personally demanding. Like most kinds of teaching, it depends on what we know and who we are. An effective teacher in any classroom and perhaps especially in the arts, is always an agent of change and not merely a transmission device. The teachers in this book are unlikely to turn their classrooms into a grave-yard of the imagination or a de-contextualised skills factory. Instead, they place participation and collaboration at the heart of their work. Students are encouraged to take control of their own learning and teachers enter the class-room as creative beings themselves. The ability of these teachers to anticipate a range of possibilities and consequences is impressive. They take risks and relinquish a degree of control as their students' responses and initiatives carry the work forward. As they explore ideas and discover connections, the students' engagement and motivation move the drama towards unexpected outcomes. Readers will indeed find the range and flexibility of the work described inspiring.

It is particularly pleasing that this book and the teachers who have contri-buted to it have all been associated with London Drama. For more than 60 years this influential organisation has supported and motivated drama teachers, advancing their practice and deepening their understanding of the principles underlying the work. Like many others, my professional develop-ment was nurtured by London Drama. The Inner London Education

Authority's Drama Inspectorate in the 1970s and 80s, Geoffrey Hodson and Maureen Price, aided by the indefatigable Win Bayliss, placed London Drama at the heart of their work in improving drama teaching across the ILEA's thirteen boroughs. That London Drama is still flourishing is evident not just in this book but in the impressive list of courses and resources in the organisation's website.

Cecily O'Neill
August 2010

On being inspired through drama

Introduction
A Good Place to Be
John Coventon

It was to become one of those 'where were you when…' moments. I was on stage, rehearsing my small part in the school production of *The Government Inspector* while a friend in the wings was desperately trying to draw my attention to the transistor radio he held in his hand. Eventually I was so distracted I hissed at him, 'what do you want?' His reply justified his agitation. 'President Kennedy's been shot.' The date was Friday 22 November 1963. The news was transmitted to Mr Benson, the teacher directing the play from the centre of the school hall. Rehearsal ended as we tried to comprehend the news from across the Atlantic. Real life had overtaken our efforts to create an imagined one.

The conscious decision to make drama an important part of my life came a few months later as I lay on the school's Sports Hall floor staring up at the ceiling in a relaxation exercise led by a bearded young man called Terry Jones. He was the new drama advisory teacher for North Devon, and our paths were to cross several times as he went on to become Newham's Drama Advisor before returning to Devon as the County Advisor. My mind and body relaxed on that polished floor, ready to focus on the new exploration technique called improvisation that was to follow. I knew I was embarking on something important, doing drama in a lively, engaging way that I could handle with so much more confidence and insight than the facade of understanding created by the school plays that had previously been my drama experience.

I was inspired.

* * *

It was the second of two sessions at the local school for children with severe learning difficulties (SLD). In the first, my Year 11 pupils had paired up with slightly younger children from the host school and together they had moved towards improvising a role play on a day in the life of a family at home. They had built up their belief and understanding in the work with the help of a roll of lining paper and a selection of colour felt tipped pens. The drama began with a scene at the breakfast table in which my students sketched what their SLD partners told them they had had for breakfast. For the second session we dispensed with the protection of a drawing exercise and instead planned for an improvisation based on a family day at the seaside that would include the coach journey, building sandcastles and eating fish and chips. It was to be a whole class, teacher-led drama, with the same pupil pairings as in the original but with the understanding that pairs could link up if necessary for mutual reassurance.

The groups of pupils greeted one another like old friends and the drama progressed as planned. During the beach sequence, I noticed that one of my pupils had been pinned down by his SLD partner. As Mark, my Year 11 boy, had a reputation for being quick-tempered, I was a little concerned and quietly closed in on the pair. He was well and truly pinned down under his large SLD partner. However, he had just enough room to turn his head and greet me with an enormous smile. Mark was not in a position he would have tolerated in normal life, but was happy to let this Downs Syndrome boy take such liberty. As he confirmed in the later evaluation, that smile contained an important understanding of what drama can do for us. It affirmed, 'I may be uncomfortable, but it is right that I should be here, allowing this to happen. I am actually enjoying myself and I know I have an important part to play in what is happening with the group.' I smiled reassuringly and moved on.

These visits took place over thirty years ago. The secondary school, in Stockton on Tees, was demolished a few years later and Mark will now be well into middle age, but the value of the moment remains. It was key for Mark. From being an obstructive, negative pupil he took on a positive, leading role within the class as well as teaching me a lesson which in its roundabout way has led me to produce this book. In those pre-GCSE days I was under some pressure to set and assess regular homework for the more senior pupils. Mark's response to my sanctions following the non-arrival of some written exercise I had set was full of indignation and hurt pride. 'But we do extra work outside the class. All we ever talk about on the way home is the drama we have done in here. But you never hear about that, do you? And it is much more important than this work... this.' He held up and waved an almost empty exercise book.

While he walked off and sulked, I stood humbly in silence. For he was so right. As teachers we can never know the full effect of our work. No amount of testing and tick-boxing will ever reveal those evaluations, connections and developments in understanding the students make outside our reach, triggered by the active drama we have initiated.

In a long career of drama in the classroom and studio, what has sustained and inspired me have been those moments of new understanding that have crystallised into solid form. Dorothy Heathcote used to call them 'moments of awe'. This is an accurate phrase, for it describes that which is suddenly so unexpected, so accurately portrayed as to stun those who are fortunate enough to be present. Though they are unexpected and by nature unplanned, on those few occasions they occur, they come about as the result of careful advance preparation, a willingness to allow situations to develop at their own pace with an open mind, accepting the unexpected and rejoicing in it. It is in those moments that drama becomes great art. Space allows me to offer only a taste of what I mean. Significantly, four of the examples I have chosen are connected to work originated by contributors to the book.

- There was the autistic young man whose only response happened when I attempted to remove the poster tube I had been blowing gently into his ear for at least three minutes and was to pull the tube back to indicate he wanted me to continue. I blew for a further two minutes before he let me go. The drama context had been 'replacing the lost flute with music of our own' at a residential school in the North East with other Dorothy Heathcote students

- I was in role as a bulldozer driver ordered to flatten Palestinian houses on the Gaza strip while the householders stood as a shield in front of their homes, refusing to move. This was at a National Drama Conference session with other teachers, led by Jonothan Neelands

- I was one of several teachers wielding a felt tip pen as we sought to find and underline certain themed references on the full *Macbeth* script Andy Kempe had pinned to the walls of a classroom

- Two boarding GCSE pupils, one Chinese, one South Korean, were re-enacting two scenes from Tiananmen Square, the first being the student confronting the tank, the second the political decision to attack the protesters. These boarding students had prepared this piece and its accompanying perfectly timed sound track as a single, overnight GCSE homework. It was moving in its simplicity, a piece of art in its use of costume and the synchronicity of sound and action, yet these students at Royal Russell School had never shown or discussed a political view or sense of history to us before

It is not only in process drama that these moments occur. There was

- the actress playing Verity in *Find Me*, describing and drawing out the bubble that surrounded her and which was the only space she felt comfortable in. This was in a scene from a 1990s school production I directed at Taunton Manor School, Croydon
- the threat element of the circling BMX bikes in Kidbrooke School's production of *Romeo and Juliet* (See Lucy Cuthbertson's chapter for further moments from this production)

There are other examples of moments of awe I could choose. They all serve to keep me engaged and responsive to the possibilities of what I do. It is my contention that drama teachers all have moments such as these to reflect upon, but it can be difficult to recognise them within the regimented conditions so many teachers feel engulfed by.

'Schools need to be liberating places, but it is very hard to do it with the utter throttling, choking straitjacket of the national examination system curriculum.' So said Dr Anthony Seldon, master of Wellington College, in an interview with *The Observer* (08.03.09).

> School authorities, schools and teachers are now valued for one thing alone: their success at achieving exam passes. We have embraced dullness and so close are we to it, we do not even see what has happened.

It would be easy to suggest that Seldon's criticisms do not apply to us as drama teachers. As drama practitioners we have been proud of our traditions of empowering pupils, of facilitating their learning and actively exploring ideas and emotions through the medium of drama.

I believe we have become complacent in the defence of what we do. We are in danger of allowing the needs of the examination boards to classify and measure the range of drama skills available to students to become the end product of what we see as our subject. We have often fallen into the tick-box trap, so that for example, if the students spend most of a lesson producing three still images, they have completed their drama experience for that time and we can tick off the still image box. Well into their GCSE courses, we are still asking them what a strategy like thought tracking is. If they can answer correctly and give a short example of it in a brief dramatic context, another box can be ticked. And so on.

I would like to believe that at this moment you are all shaking your heads and thinking that I am out of touch. Sadly, these are not examples I have made up. Where is the drama? Where is the understanding that we employ these drama skills as part and parcel of the artistic, dramatic exploration, rather than as ends in themselves? Where is the sense of real learning taking place in which neither the pupils nor the teacher are sure how the end product will appear? If the journey is relevant, has excitement and uncertainty, then the evaluation can cover an enormous range of ideas and concepts, arising directly and in-directly from the sustained drama just completed. Tick the boxes afterwards if you must, when you know they have used the relevant skills and mediums best suited to the unfolding drama. But form without content is nothing.

Seldon continues by asking some very relevant questions.

> What has been lost? Why has affluence and knowledge not brought us won-derful schools and remarkable universities? ...schools have concentrated on a very narrow definition of intelligence: the logical and the linguistic, at the ex-pense of cultural, physical, social, personal, moral and spiritual intelligence. [We should be asking] not how intelligent is a child, but rather, how is a child intelligent?

The contributors to this volume all respond to Seldon's challenge in their different ways. They do not repudiate the need for examination, but neither do they place that need at the forefront of their writing. Andy Kempe's sensi-tive exploration of teenage suicide, *Laughter in the Dark,* is discussed within the context of Year 10 drama. Daniel Shindler in developing work on under-standing one's roots is working within the remit of a GCSE project. Emma Brown opens up the potential of working alongside professionals from other areas of the arts as a dynamic part of the 16-19 Diploma in her *Guerillas in the Classroom*, citing three contrasting examples that enshrine both collabora-tion and dynamic learning.

It is not only the secondary sector that provides such inspiration. Both Carey English and Adam Annand describe work with younger children, the former inspiring Key Stage 2 pupils by turning their dramatic writings into staged theatre, the latter building confidence with Key Stage 1 pupils who are pro-tected into declaring themselves in the open dramatic forum. These two chapters are examples of how outside agencies can contribute to the develop-ment of children's learning and self-confidence and offer guidelines of practice that can be used as easily with older pupils. The developmental link is an important theme in Amanda Kipling's chapter. She looks at the early days of drama and play theory and analyses how play fits within the overall context of our work for the twenty-first century.

In his manifesto, Jonothon Neelands is concerned that we must be inclusive, unequivocally placing drama and theatre together. Our business is not just drama in the classroom. Drama and theatre are around us all the time, as long as we are both observant and humble enough to see them. They are what we see in the corner of a playground, in a promenade around a park, or in the young child showing a parent something he has learned to do for the first time. It is in the acrobatic gymnastic group Spellbound as much as it is in the Royal Shakespeare Company. It is the celebration of collaborative endeavour enjoyed by a community. The beauty of theatre is that while it brings people together in a joint experience, it may also divide them in their reaction to what they have seen. A piece of theatre will never be universally admired or despised, for we individuals are all different, so what we regard as worthy of praise will change from person to person.

Lucy Cuthbertson gives an account of the development of Kidbrooke School's *Romeo and Juliet*, which, as I write, is rehearsing for its third series of performances, this time at the Edinburgh Festival. I can confirm the quality of this particular theatre experience. Her comments about the separation and negativity of many members of the drama in education and professional theatre communities towards each other require attention if we are both to make progress.

Julia Potts outlines the opportunities that the nationwide Ambassador Theatre Group has developed beyond workshops that directly connect to main house productions, and describes how ATG has sought to compensate in some way for the loss of local authority arts and drama teams that were at their most supportive in pre-Thatcher Britain.

London Drama has been an important part of my drama teaching career and all the contributors to this book have some connection to it, be it as workshop leaders for the organisation, or as individual and school members. There is still often only one drama teacher in a school, yet we pride ourselves on being a community of teachers. Organisations like London Drama make that possible and in a time of hardship or lack of information LD has so often been the guide, encouraging us into those networks that sustain us. For its continued support of teachers and pupils over more than five decades, it is appropriate that London Drama's name should appear on the cover of a book entitled *Drama to Inspire*.

Dorothy Heathcote has been teaching as long as London Drama has been in existence. She has run many workshops for the organisation and has been a inspiration to so many of its members. The report on her work in Turkey in 2009 demonstrates the attention to detail that has been central to everything she has accomplished throughout her long career. It is an honest account. She gives a clear exposition of Mantle of the Expert in practice, but we see through close examination of the tasks section that things do not always go as she would hope. But the passion for her work with young people remains un-diminished.

Producing this book has been a labour of love. It has allowed me to ask prac-titioners I have known for years to write about what they believe to be impor-tant today. It has introduced me to a new generation of writer-practitioners whose work I am only now becoming familiar with. Hard times are coming; we must remember that making good drama in good spaces has always been a challenge, but a challenge that has brought great rewards to both our students and their facilitating teachers. Then we will survive the hard times again.

This book is dedicated to the pupils and students who have been inspired to query and perform in so many different ways what we as teachers and they as co-collaborators have set in motion in our drama spaces. In the best drama, outcomes cannot be predicted with any certainty. Every day we set out on a journey that begins with, 'what happens if...?' It is always a good place to be.

Reference
The Observer (08.03.09) p9 Focus on fact is stifling schools, warns top head.

shaping
principles

What we do and why we do it

Shaping principles for drama and theatre education (D&TE)

Jonothan Neelands

1. Drama and theatre education (D&TE) is an area of cultural learning that young people will encounter over a lifetime rather than within a lesson, in and beyond school and with life wide impacts. It is not confined to or by school, success in exams or to narrowly conceived levels of achievement that do not take full account of the stages, ages and diversity of experiences leading to each young person's life long and life wide engagement and pleasure in theatre and drama. For these reasons, D&TE is a cultural as well as a curriculum entitlement.

2. The hybrid term D&TE, therefore, embraces the full range of drama opportunities that are available to children and young people. These will include: the experience of drama taught as a distinctive art form in the school curriculum; drama used to enliven and enrich other areas of the curriculum, particularly in the humanities, including English; drama clubs, school based performances and youth theatre; access to live theatre experiences in and beyond school; access to theatre professionals and local and national theatre outreach programmes; vocational training in theatre crafts where appropriate.

3. As a singular but expansive term, D&TE includes the two dominant traditions of cultural engagement in schools and in society; that is the 'doing' of drama (from *dran = to do, act, perform*) and the 'seeing' of theatre (from *theasthai* = to behold, and also *theatron* = *a place of seeing*). Both these traditions – the doing of drama and the seeing and beholding of theatre – are vital to providing a D&TE entitlement.

4. 'Doing' and 'seeing' imply the primacy of engaging children and young people in live(d) experiences of drama and theatre. Therefore, every lesson, workshop or other learning episode should be designed to offer

an actual experience of theatre through the doing of drama and the be-holding of theatre, rather than through passively learning about genres, styles and periods of theatre without actually and existentially feeling its distinctive powers. Unless children and young people are offered the experience of authentic theatre making and beholding they are unlikely to seek out these experiences beyond school and in later life. The desire for life long and life wide learning in drama and theatre comes from the desire to seek out those pleasures and rewards that for many young people will first be discovered, through aesthetic experiences, in a class-room or studio.

5.   The 'doing' and 'seeing' of drama and theatre are made more meaningful and enjoyable for children and young people if they are being given progressive opportunities to learn the 'how' of drama and theatre crafts. This includes gaining access to the codes of making and seeing complex or powerful genres of theatre that are associated with the subsidised cultural sector; which include Shakespeare but also Forced Entertain-ment.

6.   This necessary learning should be led by teachers and artists who have specialist knowledge and skills and should be based in the actual prac-tices of theatre makers and academics in the real world rather than in the pseudo practices and knowledges that have become associated with drama as 'a subject-in-its-own-right' in schools.

7.   This necessary learning in order to develop the tools and pleasures asso-ciated with the life long and life wide pleasures of drama and theatre must also be authentic. This means that children and young people should behave and learn as adults in theatre do through being actors, directors, designers, writers, critics, informed audiences and doing the real work and experiencing the pleasures these adults do.

8.   Because drama and theatre are the most social of all art forms and because they take as their content the human condition, there is an irreducible political core to all D&TE work. Political in the sense that the making of drama and theatre and what becomes reflected in its mirror are both intensely about how we are to live together (as well as showing us how seemingly impossible it sometimes is to live together). This is not to be confused with the idea of drama and theatre education merely serving the narrow school agendas of citizenship education or personal, social, moral and spiritual education – although there will of course be significant overlaps – or with what is commonly called 'issue based' work that lacks artistry and the aesthetic working of its often socially relevant content.

9. Social relevance is an important criterion of excellent theatre and drama work, but the relevance of drama and theatre in meeting children's and young people's aesthetic and imaginative needs is also paramount. D&TE's relevance may also stem from its unique contributions to the development of those non-cognitive skills which are increasingly recognised as being essential to life and work in the modern world. These skills include self-discipline, team-work, critical thinking, empathetic imagining, problem solving and developing self esteem and confidence.

10. The social content of drama and theatre, taken with the existential struggle to make drama and theatre social, makes it a unique means for children and young people to consider, critically, how best to live to-gether, politically, in an uncertain world. D&TE should provide children and young people with an artistic, critical, concrete and active means of understanding, exploring, representing, responding to, sharing, ques-tioning, reinventing and debating the world as it is and as it might be. Because drama and theatre at both the level of society and the classroom are critical and political, they are unlikely to be formally placed at the centre of the curriculum, even if they can become central to children's and young people's learning.

11. Social learning in D&TE is not, as some would claim, a by-product of technical learning, but the core. Most other forms of theatre training, particularly for actors, begin with the self and the formation of ensemble and then go on to technique. Learning about the technologies and tech-niques of drama and theatre in schools should not precede or be given prior value to learning about the self, others and the world. The unique kinds of cultural learning that come from the doing and the beholding, the life values of D&TE, will always be greater than its subject values.

12. The growth of the youth theatre movement and the professional aspira-tion to return to ensemble based theatre making both indicate that pro-fessionals and young people, in their respective spheres, desire to work together as co-artists over time. This being and working together – learning about drama and theatre but also about self, others and the common world of the ensemble and the stage – is integral to both educa-tional and professional models of drama and theatre. Michael Boyd, artistic director of the Royal Shakespeare Company, has recently articu-lated the politics of the ensemble as follows:

    At the heart of our developing practice at the RSC, there's a set of values and behaviours which we have found are both required and enabled by ensemble working. They are the foundations of our ability to achieve community amongst wildly diverse artists, as well as our creativity.

Cooperation: the intense, unobstructed traffic between artists at play and the surrender of the self to a connection with others, even while making demands on ourselves. **Altruism**: the moral imagination and the social perception to realise that the whole is greater than the sum of its parts. The stronger help the weaker, rather than choreographing the weak to make the strong look good. **Trust**: the ability to be appallingly honest and to experiment without fear. **Empathy**: caring for others with a forensic curiosity that constantly seeks new ways of being together and creating together. **Imagination**: keeping ideas in the mind long enough to allow them to emerge from the alchemy of the imagination and not the factory of the will. **Compassion**: engaging with the world and each other, knowing there may be mutual pain in doing so. **Tolerance**: accommodating difference and allowing mistakes. **Forgiveness**: allowing and recovering from big and potentially damaging mistakes. **Humility**: the expert who has nothing to learn has no need for creativity, because the answer is already known. **Magnanimity**: the courage to give away ideas and love, with no thought of transaction or an exchange in return. **Rapport**: the magic language between individuals in tune with each other. **Patience**: this is only really possible over years. Art can be forced like rhubarb, but it tends to bend in the wind. **Rigour**: dancers and musicians take life-long daily training for granted, and theatre could do with catching up.

13. Just as in Youth Theatre and other drama and theatre education opportunities beyond school, engagement in curriculum drama and theatre has to be by choice. Children and young people cannot be coerced into doing or beholding drama and theatre. Doing drama depends on mutual trust and openness. For this reason, drama is associated with a rich and engaging pedagogy, based on the open negotiation or contracting of constitutional 'rules' which are freely accepted and maintained as a pre-requisite for artistic work. These subtle negotiations, which drama teachers are uniquely skilled in, are in themselves a modelling of direct democracy in which the class as a potential *polis* imagine and co-create the conditions needed for their full and meaningful participation in the social as well as artistic life of the class as community. This pedagogy of choice has been overlooked in recent years, or again seen as a by-product of drama and theatre education rather than as its richest contribution to children and young people's life long and life wide learning.

Reference

Boyd, M (02.04.09) Building Relationships. *The Stage*

in the classroom *and* on the stage

Exploring sensitive issues through drama and the question of ethics

Laughter in the Dark:
ethical aspects of drama education

Andy Kempe

Teenage suicide declined in the UK in the 1990s. Yet 1,722 adolescents took their own lives between 1997 and 2003 and across the developed world suicide among young people has increased three-fold since 1970. In the UK suicide is the second most common cause of death in young men aged 10-24 and the fourth most common for young women. Between 2007 and 2008, seventeen young people committed suicide in the Borough of Bridgend, South Wales. Seven of these knew each other and the coroner ordered an investigation into the part the internet might have played in the deaths.

In the USA, suicides outnumber homicides by a ratio of 3:2 and twice as many young Americans die through suicide as from HIV/AIDS. In 2008, a 19 year old in Florida poisoned himself on line. When he announced his intentions he was urged, 'you want to kill yourself? Do it. Do the world a favour and stop wasting our time with your self pity.'

This chapter considers two questions. Firstly, in what ways might drama be an effective medium through which to explore difficult and sensitive issues that concern teenagers? And secondly, what ethical questions surround the use of drama to explore such issues? But please, do not shut the book just yet! These are serious questions, but is the only way of dealing with them through gravitas alone? I am reminded of a poem by Roger McGough called *Survivor*:

Every day
I think about dying.
About disease, starvation,
violence, terrorism, war,
the end of the world.

It helps
keep my mind off things.

This poem appeared in a collection sardonically entitled *Holiday on Death Row* by McGough (1979). Is his humour simply in bad taste? Or is it an attempt to hold things up for fresh inspection? Certainly, disease, starvation, violence, terrorism, war and the end of the world all make pretty good subjects for drama. In the 1970s it was commonplace to organise dramas about hijackings, buildings on fire or the sudden freezing over of the world. For me, it soon became a challenge to think up new disasters for the children to experience, so we tried to make the dramas more directly relevant to them and worked our way through bullying, drug taking, teenage pregnancy and running away from home. The problem was that building a drama curriculum around such things became formulaic and predictable and seemed an ineffective medium for doing anything other than trivialising the issues. This led to my Year 10s making comments along the lines of, 'yes sir, we know that it is bad to be a bully, take drugs, get pregnant and run away. Now, how about us doing some proper drama, please? Can we do something about psycho zombie serial killers? Or maybe, just for a change, we could do something funny?'

The Walk in the Woods workshop explores the issue of teenage suicide. Its purpose is not to preach or begin to pretend that there is a simple solution to the problem. Rather, it looks at how people might try to cope with the fact that teenage suicide is beyond their personal control. The workshop has the potential to be disturbing and emotionally taxing but there are also moments of laughter. However, rather than being flippant or disrespectful to the victims or survivors of teenage suicide, the workshop endeavours to find ways of representing how we come to understand difficult issues and situations; sometimes this may involve laughter and seeing the realities of life and death as absurd.

Psycho zombie serial killers are not really up my street so I decided to work on a play about a single parent who arranges a marriage for a daughter with behavioural problems he cannot control, in order to secure a more promising husband for the daughter he blatantly favours. The first daughter is cruelly abused by her new husband and forced to acquiesce to his every desire. In the end she is required to publicly proclaim her love for her lord and master. It was called *The Taming of the Shrew* and it was very funny. At least, the way we did it it was!

There is a lot to be said about what can be learned from plays. One that had a powerful effect on my thinking when I was training to be a teacher was *Comedians* by Trevor Griffiths (1976). In this play a worldly wise, retired comedian runs a night school for would be comics. Here is a piece of the advice he gives them:

> It's not the jokes. It's what lies behind them. A real comedian – that's a daring man. He dares to see what his listeners shy away from, fear to express. And what he sees is a sort of truth, about people, about their situation, about what hurts or terrifies them, about what's hard, above all about what they want. A joke releases the tension, says the unsayable ... but a true joke, a comedian's joke, has to do more than that ... it has to change the situation. (p20)

If the question is '*can* drama be an effective medium through which to explore some of the difficult and sensitive issues that concern teenagers?' my answer would be a simple 'yes'. In practice, drama in schools involves a wide range of activities which might contribute to students' personal, social and moral development, for example, physical, mental and vocal warm up activities, role-plays, simulations, trust exercises and improvisations of all shapes and sizes. However, in order to be an effective medium for changing the situation, drama must be more than a bag of pedagogical tricks. Hot-seating, thought tracking and still images – activities that may readily be discovered in observed practice and in the literature associated with drama in education – are not, on their own, a 'medium' for either investigation or communication any more than font, paper size, and the tools of cutting and pasting on a personal computer are. Rather, they are strategies and devices that can be employed to structure and present a dramatic narrative that weaves form and content together.

Some drama games can be played to invoke warmth and laughter while making a point about the dynamics of drama. For example, Blood Potato is a game in which players move around with the eyes closed while being hunted by a 'murderer' chosen by the workshop leader. The game illustrates the pleasure of generating tension and dramatic irony. The Phantom Tickler and Undercover Agents (Kempe and Ashwell, 2000:198) are similarly fun ways of warming a group up, but it is worth discussing the underlying dynamic of such exercise in order to reveal the close association between the discomfort of threat and the relief of laughter.

When drama is seen as an art form rather than just a collection of teaching methods, it leads us to consider how drama students may be involved in:

- creating dramatic situations and evolving characters by exploring their situation and feelings
- experiencing dramatic situations at first hand and reflecting on how they would personally respond to the events and characters being depicted
- interacting with each other during the process of making drama to discover how the same situation may be perceived in different ways
- regarding the drama class as a laboratory for the dissection and investigation of human experience rather than as a workshop solely for the manufacture and recreation of other people's plays. (Kempe and Ashwell, 2000:2)

This last point in particular raises some ethical issues. Just as ethics are involved in the dissection of rats in laboratories, the notion of the drama class as a laboratory begs the question of which elements of human experience it is appropriate for us to investigate with children of various ages and how we might do that. Is it OK to do drama around how the three little pigs protected themselves against the wolf, yet not about how children in post-apocalyptic London fight off blood crazed, child eating adults as depicted in Charlie Higson's massively popular teenage novel *The Enemy* (2009)? Is it OK to investigate how hurtful cyber-bullying might be, yet not explore what we know can sometimes be the extreme consequence of this?

In role as a visiting businessman, the workshop leader explains how, while walking in the woods that morning, he came across police and medics removing the body of a girl who had committed suicide. When he walked on he noticed a doll hidden under a bush. He took the doll back to his hotel room, then went to work. Now he has returned, he wonders why he took the doll as he is convinced it belonged to the girl. He says he really doesn't want to get involved as he hasn't the time. The teacher invites the class to ask the businessman some questions in order to construct the character and situation more clearly.

The word 'ethics' derives from 'ethos' which, in its original Greek, referred to a person's personal disposition, that is, the way they responded to the world around them in what they said and how they behaved. Socrates stated that actions depend upon opinions, and it remains reasonable to consider ethics as the set of standards, based on tacitly agreed opinions, by which a group or community decides how to actively regulate its behaviour. In the 17th century Age of Reason, the term ethics became aligned to what might be called the science of morals. Ethics here was concerned less with how people responded to the world they encountered and more with why they did this in the way they did. In drama, the relationship between these two uses of the word ethics is of particular importance. Drama may be used to represent both how we live and by what standards. It may also be used as a tool to question these standards, the means by which they are established, and the effect they have on the way we live, or, as Rideout (2009:1) sums it up, 'how shall I act?'

By this account, we should see the young people with whom we work as ethical beings who make choices about how they wish to live and how to represent their beliefs, while trying to examine the nature of their beliefs and the consequences of holding them. In drama, students engage with ethics by exploring dilemmas, reviewing choices and making judgements resulting from personal, social, cultural and historical facets of the context. As Nicholson has argued,

Drama is a good way for people to extend their horizons of experience, recognising how their own identities have been shaped and formulated and, by playing new roles and inhabiting different subject positions, finding different points of identification with others. (2005:24)

In role as the businessman, the teacher explains how he has become haunted by imagining how the girl actually did kill herself. He tells the group about websites he has found which list different ways people could kill themselves. Some seem painful, others bizarre. He reads some of these out. He has even found a 'jokey' book entitled 101 Fun Ways of Catching the Bus *– 'catching the bus' being a darkly euphemistic sobriquet for suicide. The class are invited to comment on this information and then, in small groups, they make a number of still images depicting some of the suggested methods as quickly as possible. The work is deliberately framed as being absurd and cartoonlike. Groups are asked to choose one of their still images to develop further, by adding a simple, mechanical and repetitive movement to each part of the image. Simple sounds are added (a useful analogy is to think of children's books which have been 'paper engineered' or have buttons which the child can press to give sounds to the images). The next development is to show these images at double speed or slow them down.*

The businessman tells the group how this dabbling on the web affected the dream he had in which his mind seemed to be trying to make sense of the girl's death. In his dream he saw images of what she did to herself. Sometimes these were in slow motion, sometimes they were like a dance, sometimes they were just crazy.

The group are invited to physicalise the man's dream using what information they have so far. They are encouraged to be as wild as they wish and not to feel guilty about suggesting ideas that might seem insensitive or inappropriate – dreams are, after all, beyond our control and a way for our brains to try and make sense of things that perhaps have no sense. The scenes are shown one after the other in a way that accentuates their theatricality.

If ethics are systems intended to guide our lives, then drama, like the comedian's joke, can be used to challenge these systems and by doing so, change the situation. In some forms of drama, for example the work of Boal, such a project is explicit, overt and perhaps even functional in its intended outcome. By contrast, taking an aesthetic approach may not lead to hard and fast practical solutions to objectified situations, but may nonetheless change our situation by providing new insights and understandings.

What I understand by the term 'aesthetic' is that which reminds us we are alive as opposed to its opposite, 'anaesthetic', which numbs us and takes away sensation and consciousness. What our attention is drawn to is the way in which we come to know things better by experiencing their opposite: we know 'hard' because we also know 'soft', we know 'dark' because we know 'light', we know 'tragedy' because we know 'comedy'. But such binary oppositions are relative. To a man used to sleeping on a bed of nails, a night on a concrete floor might feel like a luxury! As with the physical world, Aristotle argued, so it is with the ethical. For him there was no universal 'good' that was relevant to all situations. Rather, there exist good people and good actions in varying contexts. Morality lies only in the realm of the contingent (Tarnas, 1991), thus 'good' is always a balance between two extremes, the mid point between excess and defect, austerity and indulgence, cowardice and foolhardiness, arrogance and abasement.

An ethical approach in drama not only acknowledges such extremes but actively explores their nature. This can be done in a gratuitous way which may leave the participants or audience disempowered and effectively preserve the *status quo*. Alternatively, participants in educational drama may be empowered by being given the opportunity to construct their own depiction of extremes and so become able to reflect upon why and how they made their choices of representation. Similarly, an audience may be given the tools of interpretation and critical thinking so they can deconstruct and reflect upon the way extremes are presented to them and what purpose such representation serves. Either way, what is needed is a degree of dramatic literacy. By this, I mean the ability not only to produce or receive the different signs that constitute a dramatic experience, but to ascribe a meaning to them which is consciously personal yet within the bounds of what is commonly conceivable. What reminds us that we are alive are the extremes of felt human experience: pain and bliss, beauty and ugliness, joy and horror.

The businessman explains how he noticed that the story of the girl was reported in very different ways on different television channels. It was almost as if the reports were talking about entirely different stories. This narrative link leads to a role-on-the-wall device which is used to gather key information about the girl, for example, her name, age, family details and how she did in fact kill herself.

In small groups, the participants reconstruct different news bulletins in ways designed to position the audience in terms of how they should think and feel about the story. Four different 'angles' are used:

- *the story is told as a tragic 'human interest' story*
- *the report sets out to be purely factual*
- *the report is designed to make society feel guilty for the incident and the way it was dealt with*
- *the report seems to be an indictment of contemporary youth*

A structure for this task is given to the class: a studio anchor person introduces the item then hands over to a reporter who is at the location. The reporter introduces some sort of 'witness' before handing back to the studio where an 'expert' gives their view on the incident. The aim of the group work is to present a news bulletin in which the intention to position an audience emotionally is made obvious, even if this involves taking the presentation into the realms of the absurd. The scenes are shared and discussed in terms of the dramatic strategies employed and their effect.

By recognising the existence of extremes we learn how to manage our lives, playing an active part in finding a point of balance between them, if not forever, at least for the moment. We must accept the possibility that by challenging moral codes and the norms of personal and societal behaviour by investigating their extremes, these values and modes of behaviour may be reinforced. Is this necessarily a bad thing? The old saying that 'the exception proves the rule' is often misunderstood because of the word 'prove'. People commonly think it means that somehow a rule can only be regarded as true once something is found to break it, but to 'prove' also means 'to test' or determine the quality of something. Hence, by investigating extreme behaviour we may come to value all the more behaviour that is moderated and considered. Adherence to guiding values may become stronger when they are tested and found capable of withstanding challenge, rather than accepted uncritically at face value. In an aesthetic approach to drama we disturb our equilibrium in order to realign it with greater conscious awareness. This is not as conservative an attitude as it may at first appear. Rather, I see the fundamental facets of citizenship as involving an understanding of the values that govern the society within which we live, having both the right and the means to question and challenge those values, and having a medium through which we can express our feelings and thoughts for, or against, those values.

In role as the businessman, the teacher narrates how he went in search of some people who knew the girl personally. The group decide who four of these people were and volunteers sit in the four corners of the room to represent them. The rest of the group hot seat these characters to find out more about what the girl was like. The new information is added to the role-on-the-wall.

In groups, the participants make a collective image of the girl's character using the new information about her. The purpose is to try and show, in a still image, a number of different aspects of her personality, some of which may appear contradictory. The class look at each image and speak aloud what it seems to say to them about the girl.

The businessman explains that one of these new characters has given him the girl's private scrapbook. The group create items that might be found in the scrapbook. A chair is placed in the middle of the room and the doll is placed on it to represent the girl. Participants then come and present their scrapbook item and place it on the floor in a way that represents the girl's relationship to it. This exercise is a demonstration of how proxemics creates meaning in drama.

Preserving and defending existing moral codes simply on the grounds of tradition is at odds with the ethical stance that 'good' is contingent on the temporal situation. Preserving and defending moral codes because they have been scrutinised and 'proved' by considering the extremities within which they exist is the basis from which we may exercise our full prerogative as citizens and as free thinking individuals. If drama is a medium through which such a project can be realised, I am all for it. Still better if it can be achieved with warmth and wit as well as gravity.

I have tried to illustrate my argument for an ethical and aesthetic approach to drama by making reference to a workshop that I entitled 'A Walk in the Woods'. Initially what stimulated me to construct this workshop was a concern regarding drama students in the 14-19 age group who were working on Sarah Kane's *4.48 Psychosis* (2000). This is a play I find very disturbing – it is, after all, about a disturbing subject and was written by a tragically disturbed person. The suitability of the play for students aged 14-19 seemed to be stoutly defended or roundly rejected in equal measure. Personally, I wondered whether working on the play genuinely gave students insight into mental illness, or if it was simply that the anger and 'in yer face' power of it served as a vehicle for the teenage angst of the young performers.

I was also struck by the theatricality of Danny Sturrock's play *Surfing on Suicide* (2009) and its warning message about the dangers of becoming entangled in nefarious corners of the world wide web. What I wanted was to create a participatory drama on the subject that would consciously explore dramatic devices, such as juxtaposing comedy and tragedy in order to heighten awareness. It seemed to me that setting out to understand teenage suicide was doomed and that the dramatic potential seemed to lie in recognising our inability to understand such a thing. When I tried out the workshop with various teachers their reaction was positive in terms of their own engagement but some were cautious about using the idea with their own classes. Some found one exercise particularly uncomfortable:

> *The businessman narrates how he has investigated some of the websites young people go on to discuss the possibility of suicide and the best ways to prepare for it. He has found the last conversation the girl had recorded on such a site. Some of the other site visitors seemed sympathetic to her but others seemed to be openly encouraging her to 'catch the bus'. Some even seemed to be teasing and taunting her to take her life.* (I have since discovered a play by Enda Walsh called *Chatroom* (2004) which dramatises just such a conversation.)

Each group is given a large sheet of paper and asked to invent a 'cyber tag' for themselves. One of the group must be the girl. In silence, they write her last on-line conversation then they find a way of staging this script.

However, when I tried this exercise out with a group of Year 10 students in a comprehensive school they warmed to it immediately and fed back that it was an exciting and fascinating way of generating a script. Here is an example of what they produced:

Darkman	Who wants to die today?
Angel	It's crossed my mind.
Mash	I say do it. Get it over with.
Depression	You might as well. I've tried three times. Kept getting stopped. Will do it right next time.
Grim Reaper	At least you'll have no more problems.
Darkman	How did you all try? Stuck for ideas?
Depression	Overdose. Quick and easy. Car fumes are also good.
Grim Reaper	Nicotine. Wasn't enough though.
Angel	But what if I can sort my problems? Then I wouldn't have to go through with any of these ideas.
Mash	Then why are you here? You will never get your problems sorted – that's why you came to us. Just do it.
Darkman	Yeah! Why come in here. No one cares about you – that's why you came in here.
Grim Reaper	People are always going to muck you about. Just get it over with.

Mash	Yes. All you need is one long bit of rope. But will you do it? No – you're too shy and afraid. I hate people that come here for the sake of it.
Angel	Fine, I'll do it. But what's the quickest way?
Depression	As Mash said, hanging's a good way. Breaks your neck real quick so you don't feel a thing. Promise!!!
Angel	K. Bye. Signing off...
Mash	Silly cow. Coming in here for sympathy. We've got our own problems.

Taking an aesthetic approach to difficult issues may not produce solid, reliable answers that transcend the fixity of time and place. Nonetheless, in order to achieve a lasting dramatic impact some form of closure is needed – even the end of *Waiting for Godot* (Beckett, 1956) has a definite formal closure to it:

Estragon	I can't go on like this.
Vladimir	That's what you think.
Estragon	If we parted? That might be better for us.
Vladimir	We'll hang ourselves tomorrow. (Pause) Unless Godot comes.
Estragon	And if he comes?
Vladimir	We'll be saved... ...Well? Shall we go?
Estragon	Yes, let's go.

(*they do not move*)

This is how I closed the 'Walk in the Woods' drama:

The businessman explains how he has decided to take the doll back into the forest and leave it at the spot where the girl killed herself. The group physicalises the forest in which the girl was found. If the trees could say what they saw on that morning, what would they say?

The teacher-in-role moves slowly through the human forest. As he brushes past each participant they speak aloud what the trees may have seen, thought or felt as they saw the girl that morning. Finally, he places the doll back in the centre. The group breaks away, looks at the figure of the doll and reflects on how it has now taken on symbolic value.

This drama offers no simple answers to why young people kill themselves or how society might respond. In this, it reflects Levinas' position that in order to provoke a truly ethical response, such work must appear to have 'no ethical ambition whatsoever' (Rideout, 2009:67). So is it okay to delve in such dark areas even though we have no solutions to the problems we find there? Is it okay to use laughter to illuminate the dark? I leave the Year 10s to answer for me:

> *The workshop gave me enlightenment into an area of life that normally would be left alone and not touched. Thank you very much for touching on this though!*

> *I thought today was fun even though it was about a serious issue. It opened up people's eyes and really made us think.*

References

Beckett, S (1955) *Waiting for Godot,* London, Faber and Faber

Griffiths, T (1976) *Comedians*, London, Faber and Faber

Higson, C (2009) *The Enemy*, London, Puffin

Kane, S (2000) *4:48 Psychosis*, London, Methuen

Kempe, A and Ashwell, M (2000) *Progression in Secondary Drama*, Oxford, Heinemann

McGough, R (1979) *Holiday on Death Row*, London, Jonothan Cape

Nicholson, H (2005) *Applied Drama*, London, Palgrave

Rideout, N (2009) *Theatre and Ethics*, London, Palgrave

Sturrock, D (2009) *Surfing on Suicide*, Harrow, dbda

Tarnas, R (1991) *The Passion of the Western Mind*, London, Pimlico

Walsh, E (2004) *Chatroom*, London, Samuel French

Roots and routes for defining identity and personal history through GCSE Drama

Who am I?

Daniel Shindler

My identity and my history are defined only by myself – beyond politics, beyond nationality, beyond religion and Beyond Skin. Nitin Sawhney, from his linear notes to the album, *Beyond Skin*

Knowledge of the self is the mother of all knowledge. So it is incumbent on me to know myself, to know it completely, to know its minutiae, its characteristics, its subtleties, and its very atoms. Kahlil Gibran, *The Philosophy of Logic*

My school is a large 11-16 inner city secondary in Whitechapel, Tower Hamlets, in the East End of London. Over 60 different languages are spoken in the school although the students are predominantly Bangladeshi. Ninety percent of the pupils have English as an additional language. Ofsted described the students as 'reflective and thoughtful' and as 'excellent ambassadors for multicultural Britain' (Ofsted, 2008). It is an inspiring place to teach in.

Rabby, a former student, lives above his parents' curry house in Brick Lane. I can recommend it if you should be passing. He came to see his teachers recently to tell us he has a place to read Law at Oxford. When he was 16 he wrote this definition of creativity,

> As a drama student creativity is more than imagination, it is a frame of mind and a way of thinking. It is creating and solving problems which never existed, it's adding your own touch to the world. It is taking a challenge, dissecting it and putting it back in a way that has never been thought of... the creativity present in our drama class is nearly as strong as testosterone and it embodies every single member of our class. Those who are maybe shy or lack confidence, their creativity throws them forward and forces them to contribute. However the greatest advantage of creativity for me is, it provides a change to the daily, monotonous life and literally blows fresh air into this materialistic world.

What kind of drama curriculum can inspire such feelings and sense of achievement? Roots/Routes is the GCSE learning scheme that Rabby is reflecting on. It is taught over the whole of the summer term of Year 10. Implicit in the title is a sense of journey and self discovery. By looking at an experience removed from the pupils own, the first part of the project offers a metaphor through which pupils can make connections that are 'personal, local and global'. Bolton states,

> Paradoxically, when drama experienced is distanced from the actual, the more 'real' it will feel to the participants – more real and, of course, more significant ... the problem of the teacher is to find a way of helping the child to tap his store of past feelings and to use physical resources as symbols. (Bolton, 1995:42-46)

Taking up Bolton's challenge, the unit begins with a chair and an old Jamaican woman seated on it. The chair is an easily transferable symbol on which the teacher can place any culture he wishes to explore, while offering the distance Bolton is recommending. For example, when I taught in Thailand, I placed a Chinese woman on the chair, as China has played such an important part in Thai culture and history, which I knew many of the pupils were unaware of. Likewise, Andy Kempe sat an old miner from the North of England on the chair.

Part 1 – Grace

To begin Roots/Routes, pieces of cloth are laid out on the floor. Pupils are asked to discuss what memories are triggered by the cloth. Having done a unit of work on Stanislavsky in Year 9, they understand that an emotional memory can 'vibrate through the whole body' (Ribot, 1897:163) but 'the problem is to recapture the emotion that once flashed by like a meteor' (Hapgood, 1986: 174).

Responses range from past events – some funny, some sad – to memories of people – grandparents or siblings, perhaps – to memories of places and sensory memories of smells and sounds. Ben Okri writes that 'stories are the secret reservoir of values' and this is a key theme in the work.

A picture from *The Patchwork Quilt* of an elderly Jamaican woman, Grace, is discussed and a piece of narration is introduced

> *Grandma was sitting at her favorite spot, the big soft chair in front of the picture window.*

A pupil sits on the chair with a patchwork quilt and a memory box. She is body sculpted by the class. Another piece of narration is added

> *Tanya, where is she? Grandma flexed her fingers to keep them from stiffening. She sucked in some air and said, 'my mother made me that quilt but sometimes the old ways are forgotten.'*

Pupils are asked to record an initial response on a stick-it note and present it dramatically to the class, using the chair, the quilt and the memory box as the central focus. The open response can range from poetry to an inner monologue to a drawing. Their responses are stored in the memory box along with some artifacts such as jewelry, old photographs or a passport. The emphasis is on deconstructing the outer signs to find her inner life.

> Everything presented to the spectator within the theatrical frame is a sign (Aston and Savona, 1991:99).

A picture of a market and third piece of narration are added

> *We use to go to market once a week.*

A whole class sound collage is created and pupils lead a blindfolded partner on a sensory tour of the market. These activities are followed by improvisations of some of the memories Grace recalls as she sits alone on her chair. She remembers the huge storm that hit Jamaica in the 1950s

> *Grace's eyes grew dark and distant. She turned away and gazed out of the window absentmindedly rubbing the pieces of material through her fingers. She remembered when they called for her mother the day after the storm to come quickly. Her mother left straightaway. It was morning of market but the familiar sounds, the familiar crowds were not there. When she reached the square she would never forget what she saw. Things were never the same after this.*

The class turn the studio into the picture Grace has of that terrible moment when she entered the market square. The teacher in role as the young Grace searches for her mother.

In the reflection that follows, historical information from *Motherland* (Dodgson, 1984) is given about the push and pull factors in the Caribbean at the time and the powerful testimony from women who had lived through these times. The class completes this section by watching an extract from the BBC's Windrush series.

Part 2 – Leaving and arriving

The context is now set. Work is done on the dockside, as the young Grace leaves for England. A picture from *Motherland* of Victoria Station with newly arrived immigrants from the Caribbean is explored. Students watch a shocking piece of film from the *Windrush* series in which they hear testimony about what life was like for the new immigrants to England in the 1950s. They are shocked to hear the slogan 'KBW – Keep Britain White' and appalled by the undercover black reporter trying to find accommodation and constantly failing. Empathetic role play in which pupils play both a pregnant Grace and the landlord helps them to understand Steven Lawrence's father's plea for people

> ...to be able to see what it might be like to be in someone else's situation...we can only change ourselves, perhaps it's a tiny grain of sand but sooner or later all those grains together mount up to something very powerful. (Arc Theatre 2009, *My England*)

This leads to an extensive piece of work entitled 'Leaving and Arriving'. Pupils are given the space to make a response but are also asked to have a conversation with someone outside the classroom who has experience of leaving and arriving. They are asked to bring in an object that can be used in the drama. This is not as easy as it sounds, because many students have never had this conversation. Clint Dyer, the director of the outstanding production *The Big Life* explains

> My parents never really spoke to me about the journey or the first ten or fifteen years over here. I talked to them when I was finessing the script ... it was one of the most beautiful times of my life with my parents. When I asked before they said,' some of it was really bad and I don't want to go into it' ... but now they enjoyed talking about it. They also loved it that I was impressed. Doing this has really helped me realise who my parents are. (*The Observer*, 18.4.04)

The pupils encountered some similarly astonishing things. Siddiqur's elderly father reached under the bed and brought out a suitcase containing the clothes he had worn to arrive in England. Fazal's mother climbed up and brought down a box with possessions she had hastily gathered when she left her village in Bangladesh at the age of 14. Neither child had ever seen these things, let alone talked about them. Siddiqur's use of the sweat-stained red handkerchief, Fazal's use of the Bengali cardboard snakes and ladders and Redwan's use of the key to the first door his mother opened in England that he had never seen, all framed within the context of Grace's experiences, allow the pupils to get inside Rilke's assertion that

> We are born, so to speak, provisionally, it does not matter where. It is only gradually that we compose within ourselves our true place of origin so that we may be born there retrospectively and each day more definitely.

Their work challenges the racist nonsense of Tebbit's 'cricket test'

> ...if all the time somebody is looking back over their shoulder to the country from which their family came instead of to the country where they live and are making their home, you scratch your head if you are an integrationist and ask: are they really integrated or are they just living here?

The drama encouraged Natasha to phone her grandfather in India, who explained the origin of her name, and described what life was like under British rule. At that time she was worried because her family was facing deportation, but mercifully she was allowed to stay. She achieved 10 A/A* GCSEs.

Farzana, who was having difficulties in her relationship with her mother, was able to write in her coursework:

> Talking to my mum has really inspired me ... I have used the feelings that my mum felt when she thought it was her against the whole world ... it has also helped my mum as I was the first child to ask about her journey to Britain. It helped her to open up and build more trust in me ... it made my mum very happy and proud as I was taking an interest in the land, where my roots go down to ... it also made me feel very good about myself. It has brought me and my mum closer together.

For Muktar, who had just returned from visiting Pakistan because of the death of his grandmother, her gold watch became part of his grieving process:

> This is the only reason
> This is the only reason I am living
> She passed away, it was clarified
> This clock is now what I remember her by
> Then I thought of what she said
> She wouldn't last long.

Part 3 – Generations

The project returns to the present and Grace's relationship with her daughter, Georgia and her newly-born granddaughter, Tanya. The class writes a collective letter from Grace to Tanya that she will give Tanya when she is old enough. It is safely stored in the memory box.

...think of me as an angel that will always be there for you. Always be proud and hold your head high, never give up for it is you who carves out your destiny ... may this memory box serve you as it has served me...

In a multiple hot seating exercise, the pupils go round asking questions of four people who knew Grace and her daughter Georgia as she was growing up. The hot-seaters present speeches that get to the essence of their relationship, intercut with flashbacks of the relationship presented by the rest of the class. Pupils make a presentation entitled 'Georgia' that entails taking out and putting away a memory, using the powerful artifact of the memory box.

The narration about Tanya is read and this line from *The Patchwork Quilt* is added

> *Grandma turned her head towards the sunlight and closed her eyes.*

The class is told there is tension between Grace and her grandchild. Freeze frames, improvisation, forum theatre, teacher in role are all used to explore this. After watching an extract from the BBC's serialisation of *White Teeth* called 'The trouble with Millet', a response called 'Tanya' brings the drama to the present day, to the pupils' lives and their relationships, to the personal and the local.

Part 4 – The personal map

At this point we pull out of the drama context. The pupils are told they will spend some time working by themselves, making connections with their own inner life and with each other and the drama they have created. The aim is to introduce them to the concept of archetypes. Later in the course they will use the model to analyse the characters in *Equus*, taking their writing way beyond GCSE standards. Rubina will express her multiple identities in a poem she wrote to the National Theatre in reply to their question, 'who are you?'

> ....I am lucky you see
> There is more than one factor
> Which defines me,
> Sure I'm a Muslim but I am Bengali too
> And I am a teenager, a woman
> So yes I am confused
> But not about my life
> Or the person you think I'm forced to be
> What you don't understand is
> That I feel and I am so free

Never once in my life have I felt
Suppressed or constrained
By my religion or my identity....

In her stunning Paper 2 performance, Michelle explored her identity as a black woman in a predominantly Bangladeshi environment:

....I am no one's victim
I will not wear scarves you have spun for me
Nor the sorrow you have composed for me
I am a King, I dare you to tell me otherwise
My skin is as dark as midnight
As black as charcoal...

We can see multiple archetypes in these pupils' confusion over the 7/7 bombings.

...There are some that say
'You thought you were untouchable
But it's England's time to pay
What goes around comes around
Another Iraqi massacre found
Not a word is said
For the thousands dead.'
An old woman shakes her head
And quietly, without a shout
Points out
'The Koran says that if you kill a single person
You kill all humanity.'
I am confused, I don't' understand...
Everything's changed
Everything's different
But I know my fear
Has made me strong
For fire is my beat, my pulse, my song
At the moment I feel ripped apart
But I have fire in my heart
And nothing can extinguish it.

This was part of a longer collective poem written by a Key Stage 3 drama ensemble I was working with, two days after the bomb at Aldgate exploded, five minutes from the school.

27

To return to the Roots/Routes work: the GCSE pupils briefly consider Stanislavsky's question, 'can you picture to yourself what our emotion memory is really like?' (Hapgood, 1986:173). Stanislavsky offers the metaphor of the emotional memory as a huge house. Within it lie numerous rooms; in each stands a huge desk. If you open the drawers of any of the desks you will find a tiny bead. Each bead is a specific memory. The students are reminded it is entirely their choice which beads they wish to handle, but that whichever ones they choose they must be sure they can handle them. In other words they are being asked to edit. No one is asking them to recall painful moments in their life. I have done the exercise in numerous settings with children and adults. So far no one has run from the room or broken down. However, that is not to underestimate what Pearson describes in *The Hero Within: six archetypes we live by*:

> Archetypes provide the deep structure for human motivation and meaning. When we encounter them in art, literature, sacred texts, advertising – or in individuals and groups – they evoke deep feeling within us.

Stanislavsky asked actors to work on themselves. So I gave pupils an A3 sheet of paper each and various coloured pens. They are told no one will see the paper, it is theirs, it is confidential. They find their place, their 'nest' in the room where they will lose the outer and work with the inner. Importantly, these are pupils I have known for at least a year in a GCSE ensemble and I have taught many of them over several years. It is not something I would attempt if there were not a high level of trust and intimacy.

Stage 1
The pupils are asked to record the basic facts of their life: 'I was born, I went to primary school, my sister got married.' They are asked to think of their life as a shape. If they believe it has been a straight line with few issues, they record the facts in this shape. If they feel it has been rather messy and random then they place the facts to reflect this feeling.

Stage 2
They are asked to attach a memory they associate with each fact to their personal sheet, using a different colour for each. The example I offer is: 'I went to primary school, it was raining.'

Stage 3
Drawing in another colour, they attach an object they associate to each fact and memory. My example continues: 'I remember the shiny black shoes my mum made me wear.'

Stage 4

Using a further colour, they write into the memory the emotions they recall feeling. 'I remember I felt excited and scared.'

Stage 5

A list of archetypes is offered (see below). The pupils attach, in large capital letters, the archetypal role or roles they felt they adopted to each memory. I tell them that on my first day at primary school I played several roles. 'I was the Orphan because I was scared, the Wanderer because I wanted to know what school was going to be like but I played the Clown to hide my mixed emotions.'

ARCHETYPES – THE ROLES WE PLAY IN LIFE – MULTIPLE IDENTITIES

THE MAGICIAN – The ability to make/bring about change

THE WANDERER – When we are searching

THE ALTRUIST – When we help people

THE ORPHAN – When we feel lost

THE INNOCENT

THE WARRIOR – When we stand up for what we believe/when we take risk

THE FOOL/THE CLOWN – When we mess about/draw attention to hide our true selves

THE TRICKSTER – When we play people/we are dishonest

THE HERO/HEROINE – When we commit acts that are 'heroic'

MOTHER/FATHER

SON/DAUGHTER

BROTHER/SISTER

KING/QUEEN

DEVIL – When we commit acts that are very wrong

THE CREATOR

THE DESTROYER – Positive and negative

THE RULER – Positive and negative

THE SAGE – When we seek truths that will set us free

This is a powerful moment because by now the page is very full. It shows the children that no life is ordinary. We all live unique and full lives. It also shows them the type of roles they have been adopting and thus something profound about who they are and who they might become. If Warrior appears a lot, they have shown the capacity to stand up for what they believe. If the Altruist appears many times, they have been selfless and caring.

Stage 6

They now write a heading, The Realised Self, under which they list all the things they believe they are today, here and now. 'I am good at football, I love my parents, I am hard working.'

Then they write a heading, 'The Imaginary Self, Positive', under which they list all the positive things they will become. 'I will work in another country, I will have children.' They are asked to reverse this and under the title, 'The Imaginary Self, Negative', write all the things they imagine they could not possibly become. 'I won't let money influence my choice of job. I'll never hurt someone intentionally.'

The sheet now tells them a huge amount about who they are and who they wish to become. They can see that a map is carried by everyone throughout their life. They are asked to reflect on the issues they have resolved successfully, the issues they would like to address before they leave school and those they know they will need to return to at a later date.

Stage 7

Next, the students are asked to write three Haikus about their lives that will capture the 'deep feeling within'. They are warned they may have to share their Haikus so will need to decide whether to be overt...

> One day he was late
> One day he couldn't make it
> One day he had gone. (GCSE pupil)

...or abstract so no one needs to know exactly what the poem is about.

> I step after step
> Towards the white unlocked door
> I see them waiting. (GCSE pupil)

Haikus are excellent as they are quick to write, do not require huge amounts of language and cut to the essence. Weaker pupils do not have to become caught up in issues of metre.

Aysha's work to this point was particularly revealing, although she is not alone in expressing powerful memories and concerns.

> I suddenly remembered the day my dad had a heart attack seven years ago, he was only 35. At the time I was 8 years old. My stomach began to knot itself and I felt sick. When I was kneeling on the classroom floor, the image I remember is of me praying with my mum and begging God not to take my dad away.

Not all the students would have such intense feelings. Some, like Muktar, would 'feel very comfortable to write all that has happened to me. I never thought my life looked that way until I wrote it down.'

In a different but relevant context, Anish Kapoor expresses the point the students had achieved through their work:

> If there is anything I deeply believe in, it is that one has to somehow learn to live with not quite knowing what's going on. That is the process out of which this thing we call art arises. (quoted in *Metro* 28.9.09)

By the end of the project, Aysha was able to reveal her success:

> For me this was one of the most challenging lessons this term, nonetheless I felt a real sense of achievement as I felt members of my group had faced many of their demons. I had let someone else invade my space and this has been a great accomplishment for me. I feel I have developed a lot.

Muktar was more personal and direct:

> To me life is very sacred ... I think life goes by so quickly that you don't have time to despair, I just think life has many ups and downs which makes me the person I am today, very comfortable and confident with myself.

Dhipa concluded that, 'I am dealing with my past. I am proud I was able to let it out. I learnt that I am a strong person full of emotions even though there are things going on in my life.'

Farzana described the activity as 'one of the most important days of my life as this has opened my eyes'.

The next section shows how these pupils arrived at such affirming experiences.

Part 5 – Connections

Pupils are taught a sequence of tai chi and yoga moves with which to express themselves through movement (see below). I chose these because that is what I practice, but it could just as equally be a sequence of physical moves from *The Frantic Assembly Book of Devising Theatre* (2009).

A language of movement based on Tai Chi and Yoga

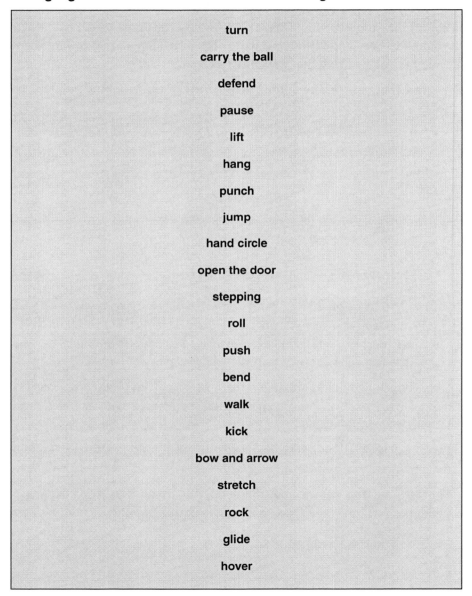

turn

carry the ball

defend

pause

lift

hang

punch

jump

hand circle

open the door

stepping

roll

push

bend

walk

kick

bow and arrow

stretch

rock

glide

hover

Pictures are put on the floor. The students label the archetypes they feel are portrayed in the images.

They make quick freeze frames of some of the archetypes, using their new knowledge of movement. The originality of their images is a consequence of the newly acquired language.

I set out contrasting paired words as stimuli, for example: courage/fear; compassion/cruelty; independence/dependence. The students interpret the words by creating a motif using the tai chi/yoga movement. They repeat this three times until they have a sequence of six words. They then asked to return to their personal map to create a solo ceremony about themselves based on the six contrasting words, using only the new movement, their Haikus and any personal object.

Once they are created, students share their ceremonies with someone they trust, but I emphasise that it is up to them how much they wish to divulge to their partner. In pairs, they create their own ceremonies entitled 'Connections'. Deep, complex conversations about similarities and differences are triggered, using the language of archetypes. Meaningful reflection is a natural part of their negotiations.

The sharing and connections made by the students at this time are a key moment for the group on their two year GCSE Drama journey. As Aklima reports, 'Kamrul surprised me as he has always been the 'bad' boy but what I did not know was that sometimes he puts on an act.' Rihan felt that 'it was a chance to see the real Mazadur.' Salma discovered that

> Abdul is always happy but behind that face there are issues...he used the journey as a metaphor. Grace would find that easy to connect with...her entire life's journey is in that memory box.

Part 6 – A Final Response

The last stage of Roots/Routes offers a wide range of texts that explore the themes, ideas and feelings that have arisen from the project. Texts range from film to literature and newspaper articles. Students are given the space and time to explore together what has interested them significantly in a final response.

Last year my GCSE group achieved 100 per cent A-Cs, with over half obtaining an A/A*. There were 44 students of mixed abilities, diverse backgrounds and gender, living in one of the poorest boroughs in the country. For many of them English is their second language. Only 35 per cent of students left the school with both an English and Maths grade. I say this not to brag but to show that if one offers a nurturing curriculum which students opt into, they will achieve because the art form empowers and inspires. Young people have much to say about their worlds, the personal, local and the global. Anisur expresses this powerfully:

> As an art form, drama captures much more than a mere painting. Therefore drama would strengthen the analytical skills of anyone who is curious about understanding things below the surface. Drama is essential for a human being if he is to express his feelings and ideas in such a way that others will understand your point of view. In my opinion if all the people in the world obtained these skills to express themselves exactly and to be able to understand the feelings beneath another fellow human being the world would be much more peaceful, free and understanding. Such is the power of drama.

Ahamodur adds:

> I feel drama has opened my eyes to realise how the past has shaped my future...

And Natasha sums it up:

> The busy lives of people keep them away from their surroundings. They become selfish and care only about I but we have to think about further to you and us. Drama isn't just about 'acting things out'. It gives a sense of that togetherness and awareness of the world.

References

1. Roots/Routes was influenced by:
   a) a workshop held by the National Association for the Teaching of Drama (NATD), based on the picture book, *The Patchwork Quilt*;
   b) a workshop led by Andy Kempe that explored the experiences of a miner;
   c) the work done on archetypes by Simon Veness and Ehpriya Matharu;
   d) Elyse Dodgson's book, *Motherland* has been invaluable.

2. The narration has been adapted from *The Patchwork Quilt* and from the NATD workshop I attended.

3. Clips have been shown from:

Spielberg's *Amistad*; Arc Theatre's *My England*; Winterbottom's *In This World*; Broomfield's *Ghosts*; Prasad's *Brothers In Trouble*; Chadha's *Bhaji On The Beach*; The BBC's *Life Isn't All Ha Ha Hee Hee* and *Goodness Gracious Me* as well as documentaries recorded from the television about subjects such as Steven Lawrence, The banning of the veil in France; Iraq; Extreme Mosques; The BNP; The London Bomb; The Bangladeshi Community in Tower Hamlets. A booklet is read which includes extracts from Zadie Smith's *White Teeth*; Macpherson's definition of Institutionalised Racism in the *Stephen Lawrence Inquiry report*; Nitin Sawhney's linear notes to his album, *Beyond Skin*; extracts from Hammersmith and Fulham's Community History Series No 11, *Sailing On Two*

Boats as well as from *Telling It Like It Is: Young Asian Women Talk (Livewire)* Nadya Kassam (Editor); Benjamin's Zephaniah's discussion of identity, *What Am I Going On About* (from his introduction to his *Too Black, Too Strong*) as well as his poem, *What Steven Lawrence has taught us.* Other poetry includes Savriti Hensman's *Just Another Asian,* Claude McKay's *I Shall Return,* Sujata Bhatt's *Search For My Tongue.*

Bibliography

Aston, E and Savona, G (1991) *Theatre as sign-system: a semiotics of text and performance.* Routledge.

Bennathan, J (2001) *Education resource materials: my England.* ARC Theatre Ensemble and Carel Press

Bolton, G and Heathcote, D (1995) *Drama for Learning: Dorothy Heathcote's Mantle of the Expert approach to education.* Heinemann

Bunyan, P and Rainer, J (1996) *The Patchwork Quilt.* NATE

Dodgson, E (1984) *Motherland.* London: Heinemann Educational

Flournoy, V (1987) *The Patchwork Quilt.* London: Picture Puffin

Greene, J and Herter, N (1969) *Letters of Rainer Maria Rilke, 1892-1910.* W.W. Norton and Company

Okri, B (1996) *Birds of Heaven,* Phoenix

Pearson, C (1986) *The Hero Within: six archetypes we live by.* Harper Collins

Ribot, T (2006) *The Psychology of the Emotions.* Kessinger Publishing

Smith, Z (2000) *White Teeth.* Penguin

Stanislavsky, C trans. Hapgood, E (1986) *An Actor Prepares.* Methuen

The Frantic Assembly Book of Devising Theatre, (2009) Routledge

Metro, 28.9.09

The Observer, 18.4.04

Links

www.danielshindler.co.uk

www.schoolsonscreen.co.uk

Practical step by step approach to a
Mantle of the Expert teaching project

Three days in Ankara:
a teaching project using Mantle of the Expert
Dorothy Heathcote

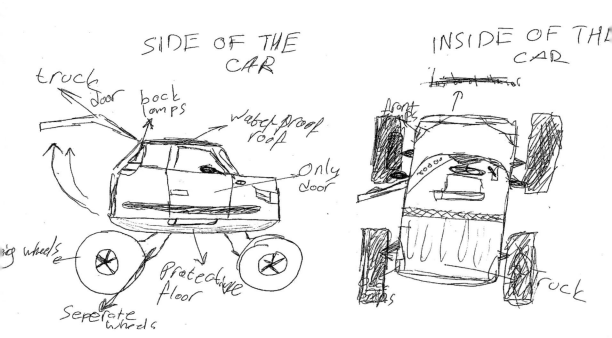

Preamble

This account of necessity has to be linear as it is read, but each of the parts contributes to the whole because each aspect of the event is influenced by others, and in turn affects the other parts. The reader needs to think of a web of tasks that I and the high school students explored together, rather than a road or railway with halts along the way. A more useful image is that of a river with many tributaries converging towards an estuary of comprehension.

This chapter may appear cumbersome in the reading. I have undertaken this very lengthy discourse because the interest of the Cagdas members deserves the best analysis that I can accomplish.

How the Mantle operates in practice

It is very simple in its basic operating structure, but is subtle in the practice of it.

It is based on the human capacity to play. To seriously pretend that participants can walk in the circumstances and shoes of others. Playing is instinctive, and when organised into its art form, we call it theatre. Between the instinct to play and the developed art form are many grades and intensities of this identification with the circumstances of others' lives. In developing Mantle form, I have placed drama and precise curriculum learning in symbiosis. This is achieved by making a contract with students that they shall take on responsibilities for running an enterprise and doing all the tasks normally required by the staff of that business. This enables students and teacher to share power and responsibility for as many decisions and tasks as possible, required by the domain of the enterprise.

The driving force of the enterprise chosen is the learning curriculum the teacher selects. This curriculum influences what the enterprise shall be. The Mantle containment cannot be selected until the learning curriculum is precisely defined. There is no emphasis in Mantle work upon students acting as actors do. They are never expected to express the emotions of persons caught up in events arising from relationships which require easement and some measure of closure. The context of the establishment provides opportunity for accomplishing and demonstrating a wide range of tasks. These tasks feel normal and protect participants into entering into the responsibilities of the enterprise, rather than emotionally reacting to each other in dramatic episodes, which process theatre/drama encourages. However, as the responsibilities of the enterprise deepen, the participants make an emotional commitment and often in episodic enactments they must identify with emotional elements.

The teaching style of Mantle of the Expert exactly echoes all enterprises where 'staff' carry responsibilities for client outcomes. Professional people in life deal with case studies. The case studies are their clients so their needs are studied in order to be looked after by the enterprise. Case studies require a degree of empathetic and 'feeling' understanding, as this deepens the quality of the task/services employed by the enterprise staff. This will apply whatever time period applies to the enterprise, ie earlier centuries and civilisations.

1. The working laws which always operate and students work as colleagues

Power to take decisions is always shared.
The inclusive language is used: 'we, us, ours'.

In the main, restricted code is employed in all negotiations when establishing the enterprise. Colleagues do not use extended code in normal associative working on tasks which are familiar to all. Using restrictive code paradoxically permits the manager/teacher to introduce the specialised language required by the enterprise. This is usually understood because it arises from within the enterprise. Because of this, students 'reach for' the meaning even when words are unfamiliar.

2. Signing is of paramount importance

No teacher/class signs of demeanour (body signing) or tone of voice should intrude if possible. The space is organised to suit the start of the enterprise. Between the inclusivity, tone and gesture, plus the classroom arrangements, the teacher *may* occasionally *slip into* explanations but not shift from colleagueness. 'We're going to need, or have to consider...' is the tone needed.

3. All the tasks must develop in an order which is coherent for students

...so the identification with their enterprise develops in the mind by the combination of jobs we are doing and teacher demeanour. The first tasks can be central to the enterprise but not require specialised knowledge. A 19th century brewery was begun by all participants taking an imaginary broom and sweeping out the imaginary straw and separating the wet/dirty from the clean/dry into located places.

The curriculum studies are introduced via the context so it is reasonable that the work or new information arises from the context tasks. The second task when building the 19th century stables was to identify the standing place of each of the huge brewery horses. First examining pictures of the types of horse which pull great drays carrying casks and barrels. Selecting <u>our</u> horse breed is next, and finally owning one by creating the name and in 'good' (period style, detailed measurements) lettering, create the names to be placed around the room <u>as if</u> carved above their individual stall. These three tasks provided the coherent development of a <u>19th century</u> stables in the minds of students.

Brooms, horses, <u>not</u> wagons, names to <u>mean</u> size and power and placement on walls have created responsibility, location and the start of a relationship with the huge animals who work alongside their grooms!

The teacher's voice here is still inclusive, but the restricted code of stable action gives way to 'helper' information, 'so we choose well'. 'The horses work hard.' 'The barrels of oak are heavy,' are examples.

<u>The third voice</u> is used when 'others' – outsiders, or people in authority – are required, so <u>dramatic</u> episodes are related with the work. The teacher negotiates these roles and, with the collaboration of the students, sets up how the episode will occur. In the 19th century stable, the first episode arose when there was a shortage of straw and good hay. So the teacher negotiated with the students whether their challenge to the 'foreman' (the role) regarding fodder would be successful, or easily won, or not pleasant as to outcomes. When the episode reaches an easement point, some workers hierarchy and relationship with authority has entered the enterprise. Now the human situations of power begin to be sketched into the enterprise work.

<u>Throughout the mantle, the teacher is using these voices</u>:

> The manager of all <u>tasks</u>
> The introducer of <u>curriculum demands</u> and
> The role 'others', as needed.

There are 33 ways of introducing 'others', not only by direct interaction(1). Naming the horse creates its existence and presence in its stall. A difficult foreman can exist by <u>messages left</u> for stable lads to obey, or their <u>coat hanging up</u> showing they <u>were</u> here and will be returning, are all examples of how roles can enter the stable 'mantle'. Some others require the presence of a colleague or someone from outside the school to demonstrate them. Remember, all roles and episodes are negotiated with students so as to awaken their <u>self spectatorship</u> of the episode. We live through the event in drama time, but we also can monitor how it is working out and our contribution to its development.

All the academic work undertaken during the mantle working through is 'published' as being essential to the enterprise records – CVs of all the employees, accident book records, letters or advertisements, veterinary reports for each horse, wage sheets. Mantle work generates a remarkable variety of such 'publications' and this means displaying or filing in realistic ways. This must be considered by all, not only students and teacher, but times when other members of staff with specific skills are drawn in – art and science skills are often required. Such team-work is a bonus and timetables need not necessarily be interrupted. A genetics input about the horses was introduced quite naturally with the co-operation of the science staff.

An outsider from a local university, or a teacher from a school nearby, or a parent can be drawn in to help. Two aspects of drama operate: the drama of the mind where the academic work and the enterprise are in symbiosis, each leaning into and supporting the belief in the work, and the dramatic episodes which students often consider to be 'proper' drama! Both involve point of view. Enterprises become more subtle in development according to the age of the class and curriculum skills required.

At Level 1. The young class look after their enterprise so all the tasks relate to what or who they are caring for. At this level the horse needs are attended to and recorded by means relevant to age and understanding. Painted portraits as well as horse names are made. Self portraits as well as horse names are in the 'office'. Weights and measures of food – hay and bran-mash – are recorded. An accident book, sizes of horse shoes are examples. All the tasks relate directly to the caring aspects of their 'clients'.

2nd Layer. Older classes can devise past aspects of their enterprise, as for example, its history and the lives of its founders and previous employees. From this, current employees introduce those business elements all enterprises sustain, eg. employee wages per hour, week and month; income tax forms; family lives; hobbies; skills; training days etc. When students reach this stage the curriculum widens and a wide range of talking, reading, writing experiences are undertaken naturally from within the context. Banking, filing systems, art work and experimentation involve all work being published. The range of roles widens as genuine experts bring experience to bear related with the selected curriculum.

At a more complex stage with older students still, Mantle of the Expert model fuses with the commission model. A commission model is not concerned with running an establishment. The students work on a specific area related with realistic outcomes. These can be school based OR relate to the real world outside school. Such commissions require attention *only* to fulfilling the task to be achieved: to negotiating all aspects with interested parties who have commissioned the commissioners. There is always a deadline date when results are published and publicly handed over to those who originally formulated the commission. The concept of commissioning exactly conforms to the concerns of current educational thinkers, such as Sir Edward Hall's statement that

> education should be related with transformation rather than information only. To keep adding curriculum labels – more maths, physics, art, citizenship, world faiths – as separate subjects will not transform. Our schools have been deprived of soul – of spirituality – a sense of the grace of life.

Creative architect Sir Richard Rogers echoes this: '[we should] use our schooling years to examine and enquire into citizenship, community, *linking* (my emphasis) physics, biology, physiology, art and history. Much of our 'quality of life' as members of a community depends upon getting it right.'

If the schools could change towards the ideas of these leading thinkers of our time, then a Mantle of the Expert approach begins the process of moving towards transformation and a sense of the grace of life and becoming an enactive and responsible citizen. Would that we might! In my three days with the high school students in Turkey in November 2009 I endeavoured to plant seeds of these ideals among the students who worked with me, and the patient teachers who observed our endeavours. So, because of the ages of my class, my Mantle (point of view) was that we should be <u>agents</u>, responsible to a client who commissioned our services to carry out their wishes and requirements. Had I been their teacher I would have first spent time creating an establishment mantle – that is we would run an agency to carry out the wishes and needs of those who require 'go-betweens' who specialise in bringing about a fusion between those who will benefit from having access to the ideas. So my plan for the three days exactly included the following aspects.

<u>My preliminary thinking</u> in order to shape the work. What follows is the precise scaffolding of the ideas. All aspects are of equal importance.

<u>The age of the class</u>. I thought I could as a stranger honour the fact that they were young and had all their lives before them, in contrast to myself. They would surely recognise how many years lay between their lives and mine.

<u>Selecting the curriculum</u> which must drive the choice of Mantle and, in this case, commission. I am a stranger to Turkey. My understanding of its culture is partly its ancient history, translated texts and its earlier empirical exploits.

But I also know a little about its more recent history and its mix of cultures. I did not feel strong enough in any of this knowledge to make them the basis of curriculum study.

I selected <u>English language</u> as a basic factor. Speaking English for three days with a teacher plus having their own class teacher with us provided a useful opportunity to develop their English language skills. To avoid my own lack of real knowledge of Turkey and its people, I turned to mythology. Most myths by their nature carry immutable truths which carry through time. The myth of Daedelus and Icarus bears this out – and I desired to use my own interpretation for modern young people.

a) Daedelus was a brilliant inventor with a proven history of success in Athens where he was born.

b) He invented a unique means of travel out of necessity, to serve an immediate need: wings to escape.

c) This myth has interested poets, sculptors and painters throughout time, right up to the present era.

d) Pieter Brueghel the Elder of Belgium has painted an unusual aspect of the myth. His painting called '*Landscape with the fall of Icarus*' in which the young boy's legs are clearly shown, holds a unique factor I could use with the young people. The painting is more than a story. It holds within its <u>form a truth for its time</u>, namely, that a momentous event can occur and be quite unnoticed by those nearby. When we examine Brueghel's painting he forces us to realise this. The ordinary world goes on even when extraordinary events occur. This is why his title includes <u>Landscape</u>.

I reasoned that in today's world, young people die by accident, or the ill will of others, but modern communication systems – email, iPods, blackberries, TV, mobile phones, the press, the media, books and foreign travel – make it virtually impossible for remote and apparently insignificant events to pass unnoticed. We are bombarded with information and the storage of it via the internet. So an aviator who today falls into the sea is on the news within the hour by satellite intervention.

e) The painting also illustrates travel – the plough-horse, the ship on the ocean as well as Icarus's flailing naked legs. And the ploughman and the shepherd represent <u>tradition</u>; settled ways of doing things, but also can represent my age as related with that of young people closer to Icarus' age.

f) The landscape in the painting reveals rocky shores, sea, harbours and the bright sun – the dangerous power, at once life giving yet bringing about the demise of Icarus because he broke the rules of his means of transport.

This landscape is very like the shores of Turkey. In the myth, Icarus fell into the sea close by the island of Ikarios (now named Nikarios). Furthermore, modern Turkey lies midway between Europe (the common market) and all the Eastern countries with their developing powers of trade. So Turkey geographically can look both ways in relating to world-wide associations of cultures and trading.

The third curriculum element I appreciated then was the geography of Turkey; its landscape and placement. So whatever I chose as the Mantle should require the students to closely observe the geography of their own country. Likewise their agency duties should include design and transport, so I could incorporate technical drawing.

A pattern is now emerging. At the centre is 'The Fall of Icarus' and the central theme. '<u>Momentous events for some may hardly touch the lives of others</u>.'

So to my context which will carry all the work:

The students will be <u>Turkish young people who have some knowledge of English</u>.

1. 'You are invited by a firm who specialise in inventions which are useful in developing countries so that small entrepreneurs – farmers, people who make things other people need; who grow what people will buy, or specialise in traditional work, which tourists may like to buy, will be our clients.

2. This firm is called 'Icarus' and the logo and message it uses is, 'What <u>we</u> build, works'. (You will be familiar with the myth of Icarus and Daedelus who flew from Sparta, and the former fell into the sea at a place near Turkey because the wax melted when he flew too close to the sun!) Daedelus, like all engineers, used the material available to him at the time.

3. Icarus, the firm, has designed a very reliable small motorised vehicle – it could even be used as a tricycle in some remote areas – which can be multi-fuelled and used to carry persons or be transformed to transport goods to markets and departure points – sea or airports or river or road/rail. (World and local trade.) It requires a minimum of spare parts and is easily maintained.

4. Icarus has built one hundred of these vehicles – their works is based in Brussels in Belgium – and they wish them to be distributed and trialled in a variety of developing countries which will be chosen by the team of young Turkish students.

5. They want this team to

    a) select a harbour on the Turkish coast which can receive these one hundred vehicles and hold them for distribution in a safe, specially designed building

    b) discover <u>donors and charities</u> which will subsidise the whole enterprise

    c) search out suitable <u>small enterprises</u> deserving of receiving these vehicles and supply details regarding what these enterprises actually produce and who would use their products (local or world-wide)

    d) design a <u>launching campaign</u> to coincide with many countries which will be represented by athletes and visitors from all over the world who will see these vehicles and may wish to become sponsors and/or donors.'

6. <u>The advertising campaign</u> shall use the painting of Peter Bruegel the Elder (1558), *The Fall of Icarus* which is owned by the Royal Museums of Fine Arts of Belgium in Brussels. This painting has <u>three elements</u> relevant to the context and the students

    a) <u>a ploughman</u> representing small enterprise and traditional values –

    b) <u>a ship</u> – transport and global interests and

    c) <u>the legs of young 'Icarus' disappearing beneath the waves</u> – representing youth, new ideas, risks innovation and the need of care and attention to warnings regarding tools and transport

7. <u>I imagined the students as being involved in</u>

    a) <u>Map reading</u> (Turkish coast), <u>technical drawing</u> (designing the vehicle) and <u>creating their work spaces</u> out of an open space empty building (a technical drawing involving calculations)

    b) <u>Designing promotional materials,</u> using the internet to locate wealthy donors, charities, sponsors and preparing approaches to them (fictional, of course!) though donors etc. can really exist in fact

    c) <u>Explaining their clients' need</u> and uses of the vehicles in other developing countries to convince donors of the worthiness of these people

    d) Finally, <u>designing how to manage the promotion</u> of the vehicle at the London Olympics in 2012.

This was my plan. I assumed that we would be working in the school classroom with access to computers and internet information regarding the search for small community enterprises. As it happened, we were to work in a theatre setting to permit an audience of interested teachers, so I knew another way must be found to select those 'needing' communities. In the end

I created about 30 such enterprises, based on my own collection from listening to the BBC World Service. There is always a way to be found!

Having decided upon the Mantle and point of view of the students' work over all three days, I was in a position to realise which resources I would require to be ready for a prompt start on the first day. This is when I particularise very precisely. When we examine the commission model, we see that the learning and teaching of the children comes through actively doing tasks.

The *doing* provokes and challenges the thinking. The doing must activate the relevant knowledge the students can draw upon from within their past experience, so tasks must be planned so as to give time for this past understanding to be recalled <u>as the task is being done</u>.

<u>My practical preparations</u>:

To prepare a CD of the commission which would detail all the precise duties of the agency staff. This must appear authentic to the listening students, though at the same time they must realise that the commission is my invention. But in fact, it is viable in today's world and could happen should a manufacturer of small carriers decide to do it.

Because I knew nothing about their command of the English language, I provided a printed text for them to follow as they listened to the CD.

I needed to provide a large copy of the painting for public viewing and discussion and this was readily provided by the Cagdas associates.

Fortuitously, I had a DVD copy of a BBC version of the Daedalus myth which I thought the students might find useful in reminding them of the engineering mind of Daedalus.

I wanted students to begin some designing and technical drawing, so in the commission text CD I laid out very clearly the possible elements the carriers could incorporate. Remember, in Mantle of the Expert and Commission models, all the curriculum study is set in from the very start of the work and remains mandatory throughout the work.

By ensuring this, classroom work and student/teacher relationships are subdued, and the 'grown-up' colleague responsibilities in community learning can dominate. It is this factor which releases the three voices of the teacher in negotiating every factor of the Mantle. Students must slough off their instinct in school (created through their classroom experience) to be teacher-dependent and to see their teacher as the holder of the knowledge.

The commission required good maps – particularly of Turkey and especially the coastline and harbour locations. A detailed map of Europe was required so we could trace the journey of the one hundred light cars between Brussels and Istanbul and determine where a small harbour with suitable landing facilities could be located. As the students worked on the maps provided I realised I should have asked for sufficiently detailed atlases to be provided too. Had we been in school, these would have been available, and as it turned out, the students became deeply involved in studying the route and the geographical details of Turkish territory.

I knew the students would be involved in drawing, writing and cutting, so would need all the normal classroom materials – thin and thick pens, small and large paper and ways to display their work. Particularly in Mantle and Commission learning, movable classroom tables and chairs are essential. This seems a paradox. We reduce the classroom mind-set but must retain the classroom furniture so as to achieve the curriculum tasks!

Under normal circumstances I would have done art work – the careful designing of our agency logo and name badges is one example and is essential in the careful scaffolding of the Mantle responsibilities. There is also rich art and design opportunity in the detailed technical designing of the small carriers.

Further, I wanted students to have the opportunity to read an architect's plan for erecting a simple safe building from prefabricated panels, and had a local engineer friend provide me with a technical drawing exact in every detail which would have provided opportunity for precise measuring and the creation of a model built to scale. There was no time for this to be achieved. Mantle and Commission enterprises are not fulfilled swiftly! Schools are in the main dedicated to swift tasks completed in short time.

Finally, I provided all the evidence of the overseas communities from developing countries which might be selected to be given a carrier to enhance their work. These gave much English language experience, as all must be read, discussed and decided upon before the communities could be created in dramatic action.

I wanted to protect the students by using a mini-commission which exactly echoed the Icarus enterprise. This required no preparation except my own thinking about the mini-model and how I would introduce it to the group of students. The inspiration for this came from a recent British law regarding the banning of greyhound racing tracks and betting on the greyhound dogs. This has released hundreds of healthy young greyhounds to be given to owners who need a companion to care for. I equated greyhound charity dogs with the car/carriers, and the new owners of these with the people requiring the greyhounds to be cared for and exercised. This latter aspect has proved invaluable in making a purpose for the new owner/carers to get out of doors and into the open air.

Greyhounds given freely = car carriers given freely

Both require <u>agents</u> to arrange distribution and carefully select the new users and beneficiaries of dogs and carriers.

Greyhounds delivered with instructions as to = Carriers delivered with instructions as to feeding and keeping healthy = fuelling and maintaining in good condition for working.

The launching of this mini-commission required only the drawing of a greyhound dog! The reason this protected the students was that it started the important process of speaking to me and each other in the now/immediate time of drama.

It allowed all the talk to be in Turkish at first, as students spoke to invented clients on imaginary mobile phones. Inventing motives for applicants for greyhound dogs permitted much hilarious invention as, for example, <u>a butcher</u> calling for twenty dogs just before Christmas and Cruella, the villain in the film *101 Dalmations*, requiring dogs 'painted white with black spots'. They vied with each other to create these doubtful customers so there was much laughter. The really valuable language experience came quite naturally, for students used Turkish language on their mobile phones but immediately had to switch to English language when explaining their inventions to me.

Their concluding encounter came when I provided a serious request for a number of greyhounds by representing an official animal caring association who came to their 'office' to request thirty dogs which the association would feed and care for, and assist in finding donors to take over the dogs. The difficult element in my role was that when donors were located, the association made a small charge to cover the costs of feeding and exercising the dogs when they were handed over. The students thought this was not in their contract as agents and refused to allow the association to care for any dogs. This is an example of how Mantle and commission systems naturally involve all participants in morality, spirituality and responsibility decisions. These models operate at the second level of styles of teaching outlined by the Thomas Jefferson Education developed in George Wythe College in Utah.

First level of teaching: The text book provides the pre-planned and pre-written curriculum.

Second level of teaching: The case study provides the professional evidence to be explored during curriculum study.

Third level of teaching: The classics of all kinds provide life-long interest in the curriculum of choice.

It is the second level which all professionals use during their preparation years of study, and indeed throughout the time of their practice. The Mantle and Commission models place students in this band because they are endowed with responsibility for achieving the client needs and requests, at the highest quality of negotiations and academic study of which they are capable.

In the mini-commission the clients were dogs and new owners. In the longer one, the clients were the car manufacturer's requirements *and* the communities receiving the carriers to assist their working lives to become more effective as to trade and affective in their community purposes and beliefs.

There were two important preparations to be made before moving to the Icarus commission. These were essential because of the nature of their position as agents. This placed them always in the viewpoint of negotiating between the factory and the communities they would locate, which meant they must find a way to a) locate, b) research and define and c) explain to the carrier providers the communities they had selected to receive the cars. So I provided two documents for them to complete which defined the two positions. One was a CV record they would complete using their *own* experiences. The other defined the elements which were special to the communities they selected as worthy of the carrier gift so these required research and some inventive empathy with unfamiliar cultures.

By creating a contextual centre to all the curriculum study embedded within it, students and teachers can have a very flexible arrangement of the order of learning sessions without the usual broken-up day between school labels of content. For example, during the careful study of the coastline of Turkey to find a suitable anchorage for a small commercial vessel, a discussion arose as to whether bringing the carriers overland by rail from Brussels to 'a territory in Turkey suitable for testing the vehicles in rocky and sandy conditions' would be more appropriate. The students did not feel that they had wasted time on sea and river routes. They began to consider the state of the Turkish railways and examined the various area of their country's geography and in particular the less inhabited areas, where vehicle testing could safely be undertaken.

It would not have been incongruous at that stage to stop, read or listen to the commission CD to see how mandatory a boat journey was. They might then have decided to write to Icarus outlining a rail route. Had they been doing first a geography lesson followed by a lesson in English composition, there would be no relationship between the two study activities because their mind-set would have been that of students doing lessons in geography and English. These gaps prevent burgeoning concern for achieving a safe economic and most suitable passage for cars, with all the human and practical aspects which naturally required attention. Contexts require flexibility in teachers and this demands flexible timetabling which at present is hard to achieve in traditional schooling systems. Time alone prevented me from taking up the rail possibility (though the students revealed interest in it) because I wanted to give them opportunity to create their communities requiring carriers, and perhaps because of this, open their vision to being aware of how other nations are developing their future needs in resolving their problems of survival in a changing world.

I only had three days and many tasks for which to give the students a measure of closure. This range and flexibility of curriculum study arising from context must be tracked for internal coherence, as one task gives way to the next one so, as in life, students feel that their study is centred in evolving meanings rather than studying unconnected subjects. Edward Hall and Richard Rogers are by no means isolated voices in seeking this internal cohesion – business-men, psychologists and the professions are all now knocking upon the traditional schooling doors, to plead for change.

The rest of this chapter is dedicated to explaining my own system of keeping track of each task-session, while following the internal coherence line for the students as they are empowered to interact with all their learning resources. Each chart tracks one session and leads naturally to the next task, though the reader may find some of these developments incongruous. In the final arrangements, students and I could work together for only three days. The materials mentioned on the task sheets can be found (appropriately lettered for reference) on the London Drama website. The task sheets themselves reflect the tasks undertaken in sequential order as best they can. The video recordings will correct this should it be necessary. These are held in Turkey.

Notes and References

1. Heathcote, D (1984) *Collected Writings on Education and Drama. ed. Liz Johnson and Cecily O'Neill.* Hutchinson pp160-170. Signs and Portents

2. The painting is housed in the Royal Museum of Fine Arts in Brussels, Belgium.

Van DeMille, O (2006) *A Thomas Jefferson Education:teaching a generation of leaders for the twenty first century.* USA: George Wythe College Press

I want to pay my respects to the Cagdas Drama Dernegi organisation for creating the opportunity to work again in Ankara. I much appreciate the silent attention the audience of teachers and drama workers gave over quite long hours of sitting. There was also the very sensible translation of the work shown instantaneously on screen, which must have contributed greatly to the experience. What a hugely intensive task that must have been, listening to a mixture of the English and Turkish languages, then typing it up on a laptop for viewing on a large screen nearby.

I appreciated how, throughout the three days, the videoing and camera photography never caused any intrusion, and the trouble taken to provide me with, first, the Brueghel painting then the other materials I had requested. I know that the Cagdas organisation really do comprehend the complexity of the form of Mantle of the Expert teaching and also that they have a serious investment in bringing the system into Turkish schools. I can only admire their determination to penetrate the system for themselves before considering ways of introducing it to teachers.

Editor's note: Space has not permitted a transcript of all Dorothy's materials and notes for this chapter. The complete transcript is available on the London Drama website, while the complete, handwritten submission will be held in the Dorothy Heathcote Archive at Manchester Metropolitan University. What follows is only the chart of the Tasks.

TASK ONE To show DH what the students are expecting in doing drama for three days.	DEMANDS ON STUDENTS	TEACHER PURPOSE(S)	PREPARATION REQUIRED	DEVICES USED IN LESSON	OUTCOMES + NEXT TASK
	Look at unfamiliar teacher. Listen to English language. Think and speak in Turkish. Respond to their teacher translating between Turkish and English. Consider their own understanding of the word drama. Find and arrange the chairs.	Examine the social health of the group – note their eye contacts with DH and each other. See how confident they are in using English. See if the watching audience bothered the students.	Placing maps in situ, ready for use when needed. Everything ready to fulfil all the work of the three days – to be used as required. Have ready the screen, DVD and player, board of paper and thick pens. Sufficient tables, chairs and pens, papers, rulers, scissors etc. Prepare the resources of the earth drawing.	DH sitting so as to place students with their backs to the onlookers, video and photographers. Ensuring students could put their own bags where they feel they would be undamaged during the work.	Students made direct eye contact with DH. Used what English they had available and accepted the task amiably.

TASK TWO	DEMANDS ON STUDENTS	TEACHER PURPOSE(S)	PREPARATION REQUIRED	DEVICES USED	OUTCOMES + NEXT TASK
Look at the drawing of world distribution of resources. **Listen to DH's English explanation.** **Stand around the white board.**	To see an unfamiliar drawing and attend to a verbal explanation of a complex topic. The resources of the world and distribution – seeing their own country placed amongst the 'big' users of world resources.	Open up the heart of the three days work, ie 'we have; many have not' resources. Avoid using a moralistic or preaching tone.	The drawing placed on the white board stand. The iconic form in tandem with the English was essential preparation.	Asking group to move to the white board, with backs to visiting audience. DH beside the drawing, using pen in hand to point ideas as they were spoken about.	When we ask our students to listen and watch we **must remember we do not at this stage have any idea about what students have understood because it is not an active task.** I realise that the drawing must remain as a reference point throughout as real learning tasks are accomplished.

TASK THREE **Introduce the concepts of social drama and the specific Mantle we shall be dealing with, using written cards.**	DEMANDS ON STUDENTS	TEACHER PURPOSE(S)	PREPARATION REQUIRED	DEVICES USED	OUTCOMES + NEXT TASK
	Read the cards and listen to the information in English and Turkish translation given by their class teacher.	Firmly lay in the parameters of the entire Mantle (point of view and the responsibilities) and the actual commission from the car makers.	Three large cards 'people' 'together' 'sorting things out'	Laying out the three cards so all could easily see and developing the basic ideas of the commission as they examine the cards.	They attended courteously, but I must still remember that transmission teaching tends to suppress any questioning which students may have. No opportunity to frame for themselves at this stage. They remain amiable!

TASK FOUR **Listen to the invented BBC World Service broadcast and, if they wish, read the printed text alongside.** **A CD recording.**	DEMANDS ON STUDENTS	TEACHER PURPOSE(S)	PREPARATION REQUIRED	DEVICES USED	OUTCOMES + NEXT TASK
	Cope with a) English language heard b) English language read and c) Turkish language heard The same text translated.	Use a drama introduction – they shall realise that the BBC broadcast is authentic as to manner – but the matter is my invention.	The male voice CD recording 'as if' a World Service broadcast. Provide individual English printed texts.	Setting in words and manner that 'we are listening to a BBC World Service broadcast' and 'this will contain all the aspects of the work we will be dealing with.' Reminding them of a) the drawing of task 2 and b) the three words used in task 3.	They listened. They read. They attended quietly. I must remember it is still using the transmission model of teaching and it is time that the group began active work related with the commission so it feels like a natural development.

TASK FIVE **Create their office groups and territories (organise table and chairs).**	DEMANDS ON STUDENTS	TEACHER PURPOSE(S)	PREPARATION REQUIRED	DEVICES USED	OUTCOMES + NEXT TASK
	Select companions and find a stage area in which to work.	Launch the active work of running our establishment and see which equipment they regard as a basis for a world-wide enterprise – electronic and practical tools.	Have ready: card, paper, scissors, glues, pens, paper – any simple model making or sketching resources.	Walking between tables using the managerial voice – introducing possible communication systems for getting in touch with the Brussels firm. Making the commission clear as to 'what they'll expect of us as agents.'	I was astonished to find that all the students made tiny toy models! They even patiently made very inadequate pencil holders and tried to place real pencils in them. I have never encountered this 'play' before in any group. Certainly it could not serve as a step to serious communications with 'big business' in Brussels!

TASKS SIX, SEVEN, EIGHT and NINE	DEMANDS ON STUDENTS	TEACHER PURPOSE(S)	PREPARATION REQUIRED	DEVICES USED	OUTCOMES + NEXT TASK
To launch the perfect analogy to their Icarus work. **The greyhounds to be found homes in communities.** **Four changes were experienced in the dog task.** **a)the drawing of the dog by a student,** **b)listening to DH dealing with a customer via mobile,** **c)doing it themselves** **d)interviewing DH in an episode involving an official in English!**	To switch from 'playing offices' and accept a completely new **Mantle** but keep the Agent point of view.	1. Lose (without overtly rejecting) their toy office equipment and 2.Use a simpler seeming model where they would carry out all the duties of agents in finding homes for dogs which must be maintained (as must cars). Create a light hearted, inventive mood.	A drawing of a greyhound dog. Brown paper and thick black pen and a person in the class to draw the dog.	Introduce the notion of 'a bit of a joke about finding homes for dogs.' Deliberately suggesting and gesturing that we do not need real phones! Stressing the problems of unusual requests and 'having to be wary that folks tell the truth.' Keeping phones to protect students. Keeping Turkish language.	They accepted the game element willingly. They invented crazy and dangerous clients volunteering to receive dogs. Much laughter. Easily moving between Turkish and English. Very supportive atmosphere. Task ended when they did not permit a serious would-be dog receiver (DH in role) to have any dogs. **The NOW TIME of active drama achieved!**

TASK TEN	DEMANDS ON STUDENTS	TEACHER PURPOSE(S)	PREPARATION REQUIRED	DEVICES USED	OUTCOMES + NEXT TASK
There should have been an official office meeting to thoroughly comprehend our work duties as agents and of finding the communities. **This did not happen because I wanted to seize the moment of seeing the BBC programme which stresses Daedelus engineer and Icarus's neglect of his wings' strength.**	They would have needed to sustain a long detailed session a) using English b) talking about, **not** actively engaged in drama time.	Closely examine their responsibilities as agents in **discussion** mode.	Arranging the chairs for a discussion. Have printed the BBC World Service broadcast to be consulted.	Using the BBC programme as mandatory curriculum, thus permitting DH **not** to be the holder of the knowledge as is the usual school/teacher format.	There was no outcome as this task was not used at this stage. **This flexibility is very important in Mantle work – to be responsive to group need and developing situations.**

TASK ELEVEN Did not take place.	DEMANDS ON STUDENTS	TEACHER PURPOSE(S)	PREPARATION REQUIRED	DEVICES USED	OUTCOMES + NEXT TASK
I wanted the group, had we done this task, to take over critical ownership of the BBC printed material and thoroughly examine all the implications of being agents.	Closely read and interfere with the nicely printed sheets by underlining, highlighting the text – each doing it individually. Students are seldom encouraged to mess up teacher materials and impose their own marks upon curriculum work.	Allow each student to scrutinise, argue, explain and leave their mark upon the printed streets.	Arranging the chairs so as to encourage casual arrangements. Highlighting pens and the printed BBC text.	**DH deliberately encouraging close reading of the print and perceiving all the implications for themselves in taking on the position of agents.** DH, in this situation would be 'foreshadowing our work' so as to test their grasp of the work they would be involved in, from now on in the Icarus Mantle.	**This task was not done so no outcomes.** Students are still in the position they were in when they interviewed the 'official' requiring dogs.

TASK TWELVE Look closely at the large projection of the Breughel painting – Landscape with the Fall of Icarus.	DEMANDS ON STUDENTS	TEACHER PURPOSE(S)	PREPARATION REQUIRED	DEVICES USED	OUTCOMES + NEXT TASK
	To move their interviewing arrangement of chairs to face the large painting projected on a fabric screen via the computer and attend the detail in the painting.	Cause the parts of the painting to co-relate with transport, the legs of Icarus disappearing because of the neglect of the tool (wings and wax) and the settled worlds of ploughman and shepherd. Also to examine the coastline of the harbourage and the fact that no-one saw the tragedy.	The painting projected for viewing. Chairs arranged to 'be an audience.'	DH giving time to perceive **parts** of the picture. DH discussing it, not as **art** but as **relationships** between the established, age/youth, **alienation**, transport (the boat), coastline and especially contrasting the modern world of **instant** communications with the past ignorance of events occurring at distance!	This is like the transmission model – they are receivers of DH provisions – picture and commentary. Given **time** to respond, they still took up the student teacher relationship – amiably attending but giving little verbal feedback. The next task must be focused!

TASK THIRTEEN To view the classic BBC film of the myth of Daedelus and Ikaros.	DEMANDS ON STUDENTS	TEACHER PURPOSE(S)	PREPARATION REQUIRED	DEVICES USED	OUTCOMES + NEXT TASK
	Move from examining a still painting of a moment in time to viewing an art film **in English** giving the mythical account of the Daedelus (engineer's) life and the classic escape by flight from Knossos in Crete to the island of Ikarios near the coast of Turkey. Especially the Icarus tragedy.	Give them an experience of a myth which the BBC unfolded via a storyteller and see genuine classic landscapes with powerful theatrical presentation by actors in exact period settings.	The DVD copy, the screen and the laptop.	Some interpretation quietly spoken by their teacher of English. DH's verbal introduction stressing that engineers may build to the best of their ability but thoughtless use of machines is dangerous.	They watched the DVD, but again, because it is in the transmission mode, I have no sense of what meanings the students found in it. At most it entertained – later I may learn what impression it made towards our commission.

TASK FOURTEEN	DEMANDS ON STUDENTS	TEACHER PURPOSE(S)	PREPARATION REQUIRED	DEVICES USED	OUTCOMES + NEXT TASK
Examine two identical maps of the coast of Turkey – the relationship with the Mediterranean and the Black Sea. **Also a world map showing Turkey's position between European trade and the eastern countries.** **These were large enough for five or six people to gather around.**	Use the maps to isolate a) a suitable harbourage for a sturdy trading vessel carrying 100 carriers in the hold, b) work out a safe, suitable sea route for the vessel to travel from Brussels in Belgium to the Turkish harbour.	Create belief in the manufacturers **and** the cars.	The three maps. **There should have been detailed class atlases available**, but I had not foreseen the deep interest by the students in the geographical problems – and we were in a theatre, not a classroom.	The placing of the maps on the floor so students **worked from above them**, so took ownership of the problem. DH moving between groups, noting deep interest, absorption AND reminding them constantly for whom the carriers were intended. Also widening their areas of reference – tides, climate, range of routes.	**This task is a superb example of how Mantle causes deep, curriculum focused study.** Instead of cursory glances at obvious sea routes, they started a deep study (as befits all journeys of purpose) of the range of possibilities – by sea, river, rail or air. Landing and unloading problems to keep carriers safe and train foreign drivers.

TASK FIFTEEN Finally decide upon the route and discuss the pros and cons of the choice.	DEMANDS ON STUDENTS	TEACHER PURPOSE(S)	PREPARATION REQUIRED	DEVICES USED	OUTCOMES + NEXT TASK
	Speak in English as much as possible and respond to DH's reminders of 'our responsibilities.'	**Build belief in the carriers, the providers** and really examine the various routes.	Space on the floor to sit so all felt in contact with a **group decision** to be arrived at.	DH's language here is that of teacher/helper (**not** the office manager and **not** a fully developed role).	Through these past two tasks all the students were engrossed in the problems regarding transporting the carriers. Most students contributed throughout the sessions and there was no distracting behaviour.
	Honestly and patiently review the possibilities of the Turkish territory in providing training grounds – desert areas, rocky mountainous terrain, absence of farm animals, people at work etc.	Also by DH contributions to the discussion **to foreshadow designing the vehicles by the students.**		She sums up, she reminds, she widens matters to be considered and she foreshadows making a formal written response to the Icarus builders of cars in Brussels.	
		An opportunity for serious technical drawing which could only be started but not fully developed.			

TASK SIXTEEN Was to have been	DEMANDS ON STUDENTS	TEACHER PURPOSE(S)	PREPARATION REQUIRED	DEVICES USED	OUTCOMES + NEXT TASK
Was to have been our preparing of a formal acceptance letter to the Icarus firm to include our complete understanding of what would be required of us as agents.	**Devise our notepaper heading and in collaborative mode, compose the letter** using formal English language and correct layout on the sheets. (This is what Mantle does – it makes **purpose** for what are merely school exercises done at the teacher's request.)	Enable the group to design notepaper and achieve a suitable style of formal business language and define the contract we would have been signing up to.	**Would have been a** variety of pens, laptop, paper of different kinds – thick, thin, coloured – and acquisition of the group into different aspects of the work – the heading design, the formal style of address in the letter, the making of the contract and the formal signatures to accompany it.	DH would have consistently worked with all students to develop the different aspects required in the formal responses to Icarus, referring back constantly to the CD sound BBC World Service broadcast **and** the printed form. *The teacher here is behaving as 'enlightened witness' and quality adviser.	**Would have been** a completed letter – with Agent logo design, correct layout of contract and style(s) of address placement upon the paper – a legal document with signatures. This would have been a huge detailed task with much trial and error and needing cooperation from all for a satisfying product.

TASK SEVENTEEN Design the carriers on paper.	DEMANDS ON STUDENTS	TEACHER PURPOSE(S)	PREPARATION REQUIRED	DEVICES USED	OUTCOMES + NEXT TASK
	Reviewing the letter to re-think the work the 100 carriers would be involved in doing. To share ideas and draw as they spoke about the ideas. To cooperate in groups.	**Begin** the process of **serious technical drawing**. To **look behind** the **appearance** of vehicles to the technical aspects. To begin the process of **correct vocabulary** required in designing so that engineers can understand each other no matter where they live in the world.	Plenty of papers, pens of different thickness, rulers etc. Tables and chairs and group formations. The Icarus letter to hand as a reminder.	DH indicating that the designers need not follow the traditional shapes of cars or the placement of the driver. In other words, to invite the students to actually design **not** merely draw cars and their exteriors.	Various models were drawn. There was much eager discussion, boys and girls equally interested in the task. Drawings were, as would be expected, crude and rough but this first stage was essential. The iconic form of capturing thinking at this stage is vital to **all** designers.

TASKS EIGHTEEN and NINETEEN	DEMANDS ON STUDENTS	TEACHER PURPOSE(S)	PREPARATION REQUIRED	DEVICES USED	OUTCOMES + NEXT TASK
Deciding who would lecture on the carrier designs to others.	Preparing to explain in a public situation the special features of the carrier designs and, if possible, to use the English language.	Help students realise the potential of their carrier designs and see already that further refinement is possible. To **own** their designs. To work with icon and words (the symbolic representations) **and** prepare in drama expressive time to lecture to an audience in public mode and possibly respond to questions.	Have drawings to hand. All tools cleared away to create a lecture space. To sit in groups on chairs and face the now **audience** of people 'come to hear lectures.'	DH speaking as if it were a BBC programme where designers would be explaining to the world their ideas for specially designed carriers to be used in many places and circumstances. Introducing each speaker and inviting any questions or responses from the audience.	Students after some timidity actually did lecture successfully to the many teachers. They overcame their nerves to enter the now dramatic episode of a BBC TV broadcast. They replied confidently to the questions coming from the audience.

TASK TWENTY **Preparing the first and personal CV, using a simple format.**	DEMANDS ON STUDENTS	TEACHER PURPOSE(S)	PREPARATION REQUIRED	DEVICES USED	OUTCOME + NEXT TASK
	To agree to use their real names and interests as the skills they would bring to being Agents for Icarus.	Give them a small writing task which was authentic to their situation within the Mantle.	The prepared CV forms (note their layout – they did not ask any life story details, which would have been an intrusion on my part). Note 'good', 'interested' and 'suggest we', the latter being to see whether at this stage they would be ready to make any personal suggestions.	Carefully not going close to them when they were completing the forms – I did not want it to feel like an inspected **teacher's** task. They could write in Turkish or English and select their pens. During this time I spoke of the need of all adults to submit CVs to potential employers so hoped the exercise felt useful to them.	The CVs were filled in by all. In many cases the **pens used** suggest to me that as yet it seemed a pretend task. No-one would select a crude felt tip pen if they cared about the importance of the task.

TASK TWENTY ONE To make portraits of their teams. **This task was not done, but it would have been internally coherent to do it after the CV forms, to be submitted to Icarus in Brussels.**	DEMANDS ON STUDENTS	TEACHER PURPOSE(S)	PREPARATION REQUIRED	DEVICES USED	OUTCOMES + NEXT TASK
	Form small groups. Select some task they were involved in relating to their Icarus Mantle – eg all portrayed using mobile phones in the dog agency, eg examining the coastline of Turkey or eg designing the carriers. All these would follow work they had actually done.	Cause them to get behind appearances to discover values to discover values **without** them being embarrassed by needing to act or declare their personal values. The values related with the office portraits, **not** their real lives.	Spaces for groups so tables and chairs would have been cleared for making the portraits in **still life** begins the process of self - spectating their work. Creating the small papers of the different levels of values to be used with pins.	Helping the small groups to think 'photograph', to hold their different poses in still form and select the task their portrait would indicate. Encourage the portraits by DH speaking, 'when I look at this photograph I see' and avoiding any eye contact or using names other than 'there is one who...'	Had we been able to do the portrait exercise, I would have spoken as a representative of Icarus in Brussels as if I was looking at photographs submitted by agents and commenting on their evidence of work done. This would have been a role episode by an Icarus employee.

TASK TWENTY TWO See if having written a personal CV, each student could then symbolically represent it visually on a large sheet of paper.	DEMANDS ON STUDENTS	TEACHER PURPOSE(S)	PREPARATION REQUIRED	DEVICES USED	OUTCOMES + NEXT TASK
	Receive the paper and pens and sit in isolated space while considering the important aspects of their lives and envisioning how to lay the images on the paper.	Allow the students time to discover the important elements in their own lives and see if they could find the form of the declaration on the art paper.	The large coloured sheets. The variously coloured pens. Space on the floor.	Allowing the students to choose which colours of paper and pens they would use.	This task revealed the individual nature of each student.
				Assist in making each person find a personal space.	Most of them were able to turn ideas and represent them as symbols.
	To take trouble to shape ideas on paper. To reveal in art their values.			Reply to any questions as they arose.	The least mature drew their interests as objects with no inter-connectedness.
				Not to intrude on their picture making unless invited to do so.	All were willing and 'comfortable' in this task.

TASK TWENTY THREE	DEMANDS ON STUDENTS	TEACHER PURPOSE(S)	PREPARATION REQUIRED	DEVICES USED	OUTCOMES + NEXT TASK
Begin the process of inventing and becoming responsible for selecting the communities of their choice.	To read 32 cards indicating 'communities who could use an Icarus carrier.' Written in English.	Introduce news of others living in places far distant from Turkey. Give time for reading all the cards and community stories.	The tables all spread out and the cards written, ready to be read. Pens provided to be used in next task.	Placing each card in isolation from those on each side. DH talking as a representative of Icarus. 'We have heard of these communities you agents can look into to choose the first people to have a carrier from us.'	They willingly read all the community cards and moved around quietly looking at each one. This would foreshadow their selecting which they will support.

TASK TWENTY FOUR Make their choices from among all the many cards.	DEMANDS ON STUDENTS	TEACHER PURPOSE(S)	PREPARATION REQUIRED	DEVICES USED	OUTCOMES + NEXT TASK
	Holding a pen to browse all the cards again and put a tick on any cards each agent considers suitably needy for wheels.	Get consensus without lengthy argument at this early stage.	The spread cards and a coloured pen for each student to mark the cards of their choice – as many as they wished.	DH standing back – not indicating any preference for choices, but noting verbally any card which was collecting ticks. This writing begins to have an iconic appearance, revealing supporters by the number of ticks.	Examine the number of ticks and be able to see which were popular choices. This is a very efficient way in which to reveal how consensus of choice begins to emerge.

TASK TWENTY FIVE Explain to each other in English why they support one community choice.	DEMANDS ON STUDENTS	TEACHER PURPOSE(S)	PREPARATION REQUIRED	DEVICES USED	OUTCOMES + NEXT TASK
	To select their individual community, speak their personal views about what use/s that community would find for a carrier and describe how they envisage the carriers be put to use by the receiving community.	See which communities were selected and assess the genuine agreement of the class. Note if they really listened to each other's assessments of the needs of the communities.	Gaining the attention of all the group. Taking away each community card which had no (or obviously too few) ticks.	**Asking the students** to remove any community cards and leaving only the 'popular' choices, so **they** take the action to remove card/ community symbols.	Only four communities are left on the tables so the way is clear for these **symbolic** cards to be envisaged as communities of working people. Words have to become images.

TASK TWENTY SIX **Decide which students were prepared to support each community to receive a car.**	DEMANDS ON STUDENTS	TEACHER PURPOSE(S)	PREPARATION REQUIRED	DEVICES USED	OUTCOMES + NEXT TASK
	Declare their choice and form themselves into groups. There were four communities. Each group to take ownership of the card describing the community need.	Get the groups organised with the least interference from DH.	Locate the work stations of each group so the process of envisioning communities could begin.	Try in language to help students tap into their dramatic imagination so that the working community could be demonstrated in action. Role taking and working in drama time.	Groups became involved in creating a 'moment' when the needs of the community would be 'stood up' as a drama. **DH now knows which four chamber theatre texts she must write after class ready for morning.**

TASK TWENTY SEVEN	DEMANDS ON STUDENTS	TEACHER PURPOSE(S)	PREPARATION REQUIRED	DEVICES USED	OUTCOMES + NEXT TASK
Shape a final presentation of a community in need of a carrier.	Collaborate and build up a way to show the members of each of the communities. Stand up and try them out in action. **Empathise** with unknown communities and reveal their concern for the people they were to represent.	Assess the depth and seriousness of the students' empathy and 'wear the shoes of people other than themselves.'	Space to work on their scenes.	DH observing levels of commitment of each student. Helping to shape the **form** of the presentations by modelling and helping students look into the lives of the selected communities. To implant the notion that all students would be participating in each of the four presentations.	Four specific and different community life styles and needs began to emerge. Sufficient for DH to prepare the chamber theatre texts to be translated into Turkish.

TASK TWENTY EIGHT	DEMANDS ON STUDENTS	TEACHER PURPOSE(S)	PREPARATION REQUIRED	DEVICES USED	OUTCOMES + NEXT TASK
This task could not be done because DH judged that attitudes and empathy was not yet mature enough to try. This task would exactly copy task 21, but must relate to the invented community.	Select a portrait of the community at work on a task in their own lives. Use empathy and imagination and **become less self-interested.**	See if students could identify at a worthwhile level with other human situations and attitudes.	Choosing each portrait situation. Providing the short statement which would record the levels of commitment to the invented communities.	Handing out the 'levels' as they emerged. To ask the five questions and receive each student reply. Assist groups to become interested in each others' communities and foreshadow that 'tomorrow we all work in each of the four communities.'	**There were no outcomes** because I did not judge that students (a few only) could summon the caring energy to make this challenge work to positive ends for all the group. Two or three 'distractor students' emerged.

TASK TWENTY NINE	DEMANDS ON STUDENTS	TEACHER PURPOSE(S)	PREPARATION REQUIRED	DEVICES USED	OUTCOMES + NEXT TASK
Student groups each demonstrated how their community would be demonstrated in full drama mode – using the English chamber texts DH wrote during her lunch break. **Translations will be provided later.**	De-centre from their own lives and take over and **care about** the needs of others in distant parts. Demonstrate one community and attend to watching three others.	Discover how ready students were to identify with other lives. This is the climaxing point of all the previous tasks and the **heart** of the Mantle commission. Create the Chamber Theatre texts to be used.	Clear space to show each community in action and space for the watchers. Promises that Turkish translations will be available eventually.	To foreshadow that 'tomorrow we shall all take part in demonstrating each community need of a carrier to the Icarus representative in Brussels.'	Achievement was at low level because of distracting behaviour of some of the students. These were so intrusive that DH issued an ultimatum regarding the next day's work. **This is not a useful thing to do!**

TASK THIRTY	DEMANDS ON STUDENTS	TEACHER PURPOSE(S)	PREPARATION REQUIRED	DEVICES USED	OUTCOMES + NEXT TASK
Listen to DH's assessment of the quality of the emerging work. **Hand back the texts so they can be copied and translated for next day.**	Attend to DH's words or ignore them. Make their decisions as individuals whether to attend class next day. (As it was a volunteer class they had the choice.)	Stress the importance of empathy in humans so as to release caring responsibility, ethical behaviour and attention to the needs of others.	Collect the students together, standing up around DH.	DH demonstrating her disappointment in the levels of some student behaviour. Make it clear that they would have to choose whether to attend the next day's class work. If possible, help them understand that drama requires empathy and serious thought.	Uncertain as to whether students would choose to come to class next day! DH must prepare the four chamber theatre texts whether or not students come to class, because the audience of teachers could be used to learn about this form of theatre.

TASK THIRTY ONE **Work in detail on all four texts and all the students to participate in each one.**	DEMANDS ON STUDENTS	TEACHER PURPOSE(S)	PREPARATION REQUIRED	DEVICES USED	OUTCOMES + NEXT TASK
	Come to class in spite of DH's ultimatum of the preview afternoon – 'to return and work seriously or decide not to come to class.'	Work with students to achieve the creation of other communities and demonstrate that they could attend to people's lives in other areas of the world.	Providing all the chamber texts for all four groups.	DH clarifying the differences between all four episodes. **The tree saplings** dealt with **prejudice against new ways to** do things. The batik factory demonstrated the **heaviness of the cloths to be lifted by** humans. The doctor sequence demonstrated the stress on the sick **and the weight of the responsibility** carried by the lone doctor. The water sequence demonstrated the **vulnerability of women when treated as objects.**	All the students arrived! And in the main they sustained the work and tried to use the chamber theatre texts well. They came with positive attitudes and toleration of DH's adverse comments after Task 30! They were indeed forgiving of her critique of their work.

TASK	DEMANDS ON STUDENTS	TEACHER PURPOSE(S)	PREPARATION REQUIRED	DEVICES USED	OUTCOMES + NEXT TASK
THIRTY TWO to THIRTY FIVE **Working out in detail the dramatic texts to the best of their ability in a very short time span.**	Accept the teacher's texts. Choose to use English **or** Turkish. Expose themselves as interpreters in immediate drama time by making the ideas demonstrated. Generously support each of the communities and participate in all of them. Work long hours without breaks.	Achieve **for** the students the four pieces of theatre. Try to show them how theatre works efficiently to reveal many pressures on people simultaneously. Help them achieve a closure of sorts to their three days work.	Having the translated texts available for all. These were hastily done by helpful teachers and needed further work regarding the poetic style of DH's narrative style.	Working fully as director/helper to bring out the students' own ideas in working out the texts in action. Helping them to feel and **see** that their ideas could be incorporated into the final forms they produced.	All four community plays achieved and students became involved with their statements in theatre form. They tolerated the pressures DH laid on them to shape the ideas, **but they did not wish then to re-demonstrate the episodes to DH who would have represented the Icarus firm to deepen the work by questioning in role.** Sadly, an opportunity missed!

The school play from rehearsal to Riverside Studios

Throw your mistempered weapons to the ground

An account of rehearsals for *Romeo and Juliet* performed by Kidbrooke School at Greenwich Theatre and Riverside Studios

Lucy Cuthbertson

We are in an early rehearsal for our production of *Romeo and Juliet* and we are exploring the role of the Nurse. We have decided that our production is to have a modern context and in particular a scenario of social deprivation. This is not a likely situation for a live-in wet nurse or even a nanny to be employed, so who can this character realistically be if we are to update the setting but not radically alter the original sense of her relationship to the Capulet family? We are doing this work as a whole company. At this stage students have been through two stages of auditions to join the cast but individual roles are not yet cast.

The whole company divide into groups of three and come up with their own versions of Act 1 Scene 3, where we first meet the Nurse, Lady Capulet and Juliet. By the end of this rehearsal, we have a collective idea of what is working and what we might want to keep. We all feel more familiar with this scene, though ultimately it will only require three of the company in performance. Everyone is contributing to the debate on how the play will ultimately turn out.

Mid-March 2009 is the deadline. Our production is programmed for a week at Greenwich Theatre – seven performances in all, including two free matinees for local schools in Greenwich. It is likely to sell out. We have a strong track record as a drama department for our productions. Our *Hamlet* won the Schools' Shakespeare Drama Festival and performed at the Duke of York's; *Just* by Ali Smith was chosen by NT Connections to perform at the Olivier Theatre; the world premiere adaptation of *Hotel World*, Ali Smith's Booker shortlisted novel, was performed at Greenwich Theatre and the Edinburgh Festival and won the Fringe Review Best Play Award 2008. An all boys production of *Galatea* by John Lyly was performed in the Painted Hall at the Royal Naval College, where it had not been seen since it was performed in front of Queen Elizabeth I in 1588! We are in an unusual, probably unique situation for a school. There can be no question of producing something that looks like a school play, even a good school play – we are aiming for something of professional standard that happens to be performed by young people.

At first we meet only once a week for a couple of hours after school – the production week is still six months off. This is a luxurious situation that many directors in the professional world long for – a Peter Brook method of working! All the rehearsals take place in our own time until just before the week in Greenwich Theatre. The early sessions are spent trying to find out whether the interpretation idea I present to the company will work and what their first responses will be.

Romeo and Juliet was never a play I had much interest in directing. Although I am passionate about directing Shakespeare and have done so many times professionally and for a school and although I had seen numerous productions of the play over the years, none were memorable, which is a tragedy in itself when you strip the play down to the basic plot. Two young people kill themselves at the end of a story in which we have seen three other young people die senselessly, all as the result of family-based gang violence. I felt the play should be devastating and yet somehow it never was.

The main characters in some productions were hard to like, even irritating, making their dilemmas difficult to sympathise with; the fighting could be half-hearted, the deaths made romantic, and often everyone was just *too old* – actors pushing thirty who perhaps felt they could just squeeze in playing Romeo before it was too late. There was a production at the Globe a few years back where Verona gang membership appeared to be exclusively open to the over-forties. It was not the stuff to excite and inspire our next generation of theatregoers or challenge many of their negative pre-conceptions of the relevance of Shakespeare to their own lives. Given that a large majority of our audience would be young people, many who were studying the play or seeing Shakespeare for the first time, it was vital that the interpretation and staging of the play appealed to them.

Romeo and Juliet can be viewed as an early example of a play which has as its main theme a strong anti-knife, anti-gang message. If we made that the focus of our interpretation and really drew out this aspect of the plot, what could be more relevant today? With the current climate of street violence and the spate of gang related killings of young people in Britain and particularly London, it felt impossible and ultimately pointless to tackle the play without addressing that reality. So this became one of our challenges – to do Shakespeare's play but to set it in contemporary south London.

This dictated the main aspect in which our interpretation would differ from the original – our Montague and Capulet families would be placed low down the social and economic scale. We wanted to depict gang related violence realistically, in a way that would invite the audience to question it. The idle rich taking part in 'new mutiny' would hold less relevance to young people in contemporary society where gang membership is most commonly a sign of poverty, lack of aspiration, exclusion from school and other indicators of deprivation. How we would actually portray this violence is described later.

Returning to rehearsals and the question of the Nurse, we eventually decide to stop complicating the issue ('Miss, could she be a nurse stripper-gram?')

and simply play her as a nurse – that is her job. We imagine a plausible back-story where she has lived next door to the Capulet family for many years, effectively bringing Juliet up through this close association. Given that Lady Capulet was a teenage mother: 'I was your mother much upon these years that you are now a maid,' a situation not uncommon in areas of social deprivation, the parenting help would have been much needed. The Nurse is always in her uniform – we feel certain she does long shifts at a local hospital.

All these ideas are thought up, played with and the best and most appropriate for the production are built in incrementally. We feel we have a solution to the issue of who the nurse is in our production whilst trying to be rigorous about integrity to the text. I am not interested in twisting a script to fit an unrelated interpretation – the aim is to illuminate the play through a fresh version whilst also drawing out one of the main themes most relevant to a present-day audience. This slow workshopping approach to creating a play also results in the ideal casting revealing itself as part of the process. The students have not yet been assigned their specific roles, partly so we can focus on the whole concept and ensemble work, together developing a commitment to the interpretation without the distraction of knowing individual parts. The extra benefit of this is that the actors play around freely and unselfconsciously with multiple roles and the best casting tends to emerge. By the time this is finalised just before the Christmas holiday, we all agree that Billy, a 13-year-old boy, is perfect for the Nurse and there is a similar consensus over the other roles.

Romeo and Juliet ends with a double suicide and the recent events in Bridgend were fresh in our minds. Local people were reported as saying that after some twenty young people had taken their own lives over a period of eighteen months, suicide now just seemed 'normal, fashionable almost'. The local Bridgend papers described their youngsters as 'romanticising suicide' in the same way that I felt many productions did over the fate of Romeo and Juliet. There may indeed be an element of romance to some suicides, perhaps also a moment of posthumous fame, but then a day later, a week later, a year later, that person is still dead. This was the reality I wanted to communicate clearly – an ending that was hopeless, shocking and dramatic: about dead young people and wasted lives. The production would be shown to huge numbers of young people. We needed to be very clear about which messages we were choosing to present about life and death. I knew I wanted it to end with body bags – anti-glamour, anti-romance – the reality of what it means to be dead.

Several youths had already been killed on London's streets in 2008 when we started rehearsing that autumn. Carrying a knife or some kind of weapon was becoming an essential accessory amongst young people, especially boys, whether they felt it necessary or just cool. The official line from the police and the government was that carrying a knife made you more likely to be a victim of knife-crime yourself. Some of the campaign posters showed the horrific injuries caused by a knife attack.

One gang murder in Kennington had stuck with me and seemed to suggest a way into the violence of the play. A couple of years before, a 16 years old youth, Abukar Mahumed, was killed after he was chased by half a dozen hooded youngsters on bikes, bandanas covering their faces. They surrounded and shot him, execution style, before cycling away. There were also the images of the killer of 11 year old Rhys Jones, caught on CCTV cycling away from the scene. It was becoming familiar – gangs of young people, bandanas over their faces like highwaymen, too young to hold a driving licence, using bikes in crimes and as a means of getaway. This felt right for our Capulets.

Rehearsals continue and little by little we piece together the world of our play, always pooling ideas, and things slowly fall into place. The interpretation starts to have a life of its own and generally works harmoniously with the text.

A girl plays the role of the Friar. It is a character that lends itself to being played by the opposite sex and I wanted to address the usual imbalance of roles for female actors, especially given that the Nurse was being played by a boy. She is a vicar, working in the local community. We decide that religion has to have some practical, social use in the fractured world of our play. When we first see her at the beginning of Act 2 Scene 3, she is running a club for dis-affected youth, a gardening club, to reflect the main passion given to the character by Shakespeare. Later on she is running a basketball club.

Four BMX bikes are introduced into rehearsals. I knew early on that I wanted this to be Mercutio's fate – a gang arriving one by one on bikes and slowly circling him until the fight kicks off and he is killed. We decide to echo this in the very opening moments of the play – a random youth on his phone, sur-rounded by a hooded BMX gang, robbed and kicked senseless – so that when Benvolio utters the chilling line 'by my head, here come the Capulets' as the first bike enters, the audience can anticipate what is coming. We find that the simple act of three or four bikes silently circling a victim is terrifying to watch – the wheels make a whirring sound that is menacing. The students have to cycle quite slowly for safety purposes but this only increases the sense of threat – the whole thing feels like sharks moving in before an attack. It reminds me of how important it is to get props into rehearsals early; you discover things by experimenting that you could never predict. I have been a cyclist for years but had never really heard the noise the wheels make until we experimented with this scene in the drama hall.

Bikes flit across the stage at unexpected moments, they become a constant presence. Two cross the stage during the balcony scene – disturbing the conversation between Romeo and Juliet. It gives a real sense of danger, a reminder to Romeo that, as Juliet warns him, 'if they see you they will murder you.'

The hoodie will be the main costume design for our production. We decide on different colours for the Capulets and Montagues. On the back of theirs, the Capulets have a logo of a roaring tiger: Tybalt is described as 'the king of cats' and the Montagues have a tag design postcode logo that is a cross between Verona and Woolwich: VR18. The appeal of the hoodie, according to Angela McRobbie, professor of communications at Goldsmiths College, is 'its promise of anonymity, mystery and anxiety'. We do a workshop session on 'hoodie behaviour' for a couple of hours. There is some discovery about how wearing a hood makes you feel: having no confidence about yourself, being a clone, a wish to look menacing and a means not to be recognised if committing a crime are some of the responses. I get students to improvise, simply hanging out in groups for half an hour. After this exercise they soon feel exhausted. We realise how draining it is doing nothing, just loitering without intent, how you start to feel bored and hopeless. Almost all the students in the play, whatever their background, have focus, aspirations and confidence. Playing the opposite is difficult and, we discover, makes you feel depressed and tired.

Working on the depiction of violence takes up a significant proportion of rehearsal time and it seems right that it should. We aim in the opening of the play to set the scene of a society characterised by gang violence. This is to be a fast moving, carefully choreographed physical piece to music that takes its inspiration from Shakespeare's opening but in our approach cuts all the dialogue until the entrance of the Prince. To make this work practically and to create some sense of structure, I split the company into three groups, setting each group to devise two different moments of gang violence. Each mini-scene will feature a lone victim being set upon by a group of youths, as this situation was felt to be far more common today than the type of violence, gang on gang, portrayed at the beginning of *Romeo and Juliet*. The actual elements of violence are drawn from the news and, in some cases, experience:

the spray in the face, the victim urinated on, the head stamped on, the events recorded on mobile phones for gang posterity, the BMX bikes surrounding a victim; the attack that verges on rape; the humiliation of a victim; the mugging for the mobile phone; the kickings; the hoodies, the baseball caps, the bandanas and scarves over faces, the tracksuits, the knives, the tools, the stabbings and the beatings. We find a fitting Elizabethan end to what we are hoping is five minutes of unrelenting, emotionally exhausting carnage – an individual bites his thumb at another gang, who catch up with him, hold him down and brutally cut his thumb off.

'Your mum' rhymes with 'your thumb' so it seems that the cuss comes full circle. We like that coincidence and occasionally characters deliver a shortened version of Shakespeare's line 'do you bite your thumb at me?' to just 'your thumb!' if any additional verbal abuse is needed.

Much gang violence involving young people uses knives and sharp, improvised tools – these would be the weapons of our play. However, we decide very early on not to use stage blood, which might appear contradictory to the aim of creating realistic violence. As well as practically tricky, it becomes unnecessary; the acting is convincing enough without it. And then we decide to do without knives as well – the squeak-squeak of the dodgy retractable blade and lack of any suitable, convincing alternatives were the main reasons for this. It was a decision supported by fight director Stevie Raine, who was invited in to rehearsals to work with the cast on technicalities for a few hours, for example, how to kick and punch and slap and head butt convincingly and without injury.

This idea of hidden weapons is a hallmark of modern knife violence: no arrogant brandishing of rapiers as might appear in a traditional performance of *Romeo and Juliet*. Stevie said that when he worked as a bouncer, knives or other tools were never seen – they were concealed in the sleeve, the hand or the pocket and then all of a sudden, a moment of violence would occur, a person badly cut up, blood everywhere and still no weapon had been glimpsed. A clenched fist in the sleeve of a hoodie or a tracksuit bottom pocket became all it needed in our production to indicate a character was armed.

These developments led on to further artistic decisions based on information about the way gangs operate. A recent NASUWT report suggested that some young people were recruited into gangs as young as nine or ten. 'Teachers said gangs had 'clear hierarchical structures', with older members recruiting younger boys to do work such as stashing guns and running drugs' (Broadhurst *et al,* 2009). We give Tybalt a young Capulet gang member, – a sidekick who carries his knife – 'fetch me my rapier, boy' (Act 1 Scene 5) who can take the flak for carrying it and hands it surreptitiously to Tybalt when he needs it.

Like all crime, the violence and knife crime in our production becomes a political opportunity. We feel this is the correct way to interpret it today. Our Prince is a politician and her campaign slogan, 'throw your mistempered weapons to the ground,' is a plea from the speech in Act 1 Scene 1. We are familiar with current anti-knife campaign slogans – 'Don't carry a knife; it's not a good look'; 'Carrying a Knife. It's Not a Game'; 'Value your Life not a Knife' and so on. This line of Shakespeare's about 'mistempered weapons' is such a statement 400 years earlier, and it becomes the key quote of our production. As one reviewer pointed out, it is not the most oft-quoted line from Romeo and Juliet. But it was the line most relevant to our interpretation and a message we repeated, projected onto the screens and directed at the young people in the audience in a final image over the body-bagged corpses of Paris, *Romeo and Juliet*. The Prince evolves into an opportunist politician who jumps on the anti-crime bandwagon. She is somewhat inspired by the likes of Sarah Palin, the whiff of celebrity and corruption, but her first entrance is definitely Harriet Harman, donning her stab-proof vest before addressing the gang members.

We draw on the rituals around death seen on the streets today to influence certain scenes and the overall production design: the flowers, messages, photos and toys placed at the place of death, the vigils and gatherings. A piece of fencing is present on stage as the play opens. As the violence continues and the victims mount up, the cast add more and more pieces of memorabilia until it is bending under its own weight by the time the Prince enters. We try to emphasise the waste of young life rather than glorifying the fighting. Over the dead bodies of Mercutio and Tybalt (Act 3 Scene 1) lying in the street surrounded by bystanders, screaming relatives, police, paramedics, hooded youths ghoulishly taking photos on their mobile phones, we flash up a series of photos of the two actors from childhood to the present. We want to give both deaths equal weight: both were young men who died in gang violence, who were once little boys, neither one more guilty or innocent than the other, but both victims of a society where street violence amongst young people is so prevalent.

The deaths of Mercutio and Tybalt, we decide, are the perfect dramatic climax for the end of the first half but Act 3 Scene 1 still has the arrival of the Prince and the questioning of Benvolio. Picking up where we left off, the opening of our second half turns into a nasty interrogation scene with the Prince questioning Benvolio – in our production played by a black actor – a young black man found with a weapon at the scene of a crime. We decide to imply that he is killed in custody, our solution to the rather mysterious disappearance of Benvolio from Shakespeare's play. It is perhaps the point at which we most bend the original play to suit our interpretation but it feels a valid way of filling in the gaps and is consistent with our portrayal of a society where violence is endemic in every institution. The controversial circumstances surrounding the recent death of Sean Rigg, a black man, in police custody in Brixton were a reminder that these issues are, sadly, still current.

The young audience coming to see our production watch their contemporaries perform the play – presumably a different experience on many levels to watching a production performed by adult actors. In addition to that, according to a survey we do, the vast majority have never seen a live theatre production of *Romeo and Juliet* before, most have never seen any production of a Shakespeare play before, and many are at the theatre for the first time. A large number have seen the Baz Luhrmann film version. Fantastic as it is, it is still clearly set somewhere else. Our version looks like anywhere around here. In the interval one boy tries to articulate a question about interpretation, 'who told them ... who told them to do it ... like that?'

The audience response from both adults and young people is overwhelming. The student response is especially gratifying, for this is *Shakespeare*, the genre they, as adolescents, are almost pre-programmed to have a natural aversion to. Yet they have been won over by the cast of people their own age, performing it with ease, making complete sense of it and showing how the story is completely relevant as well as dramatic. School students are the most challenging target audience when directing a play. They have rarely paid for their own ticket, have frequently not chosen to come to the theatre of their own free will, are hugely influenced by peer pressure and behaviour. Their understanding of theatre etiquette is often limited, their attention span short and their listening skills have diminished to a fraction of what the actors at the Globe could have expected from their audience when the play was originally performed. When you are making theatre, using difficult adult plays for an audience that will be predominantly young, you must work hard – they need to understand it or you will lose them. The opportunity to excite young people about Shakespeare and theatre is too important to miss.

There are plenty of ways to keep the attention of your audience. Shakespeare gives you natural breaks, with numerous scenes within several acts. The breaks in between each can be viewed as moments just waiting to be exploited in a way that helps audience concentration and enhances the overall concept of the play you are trying to create. Consequently, we have no black-outs – just music perhaps, or bikes crossing the stage; sometimes actor/stage managers starting a fight with each other while moving a piece of set; the multi-media projections change to reflect the next scene and setting; hoodies run for their life across the stage from some imaginary fight off-stage; hope-fully, never a dull moment.

We create whole extra scenes that we feel complement the play – between Act 3 Scene 2 and 3, for example, when the Nurse has left Juliet to go and visit Romeo, she comes across the two families paying their respects at the site where Tybalt and Mercutio died. We have this moment end with the two mothers starting a huge fight as they lay their flowers under their photos. We thought this was suitably appalling behaviour.

The most radical extra scene we add is the moment after Juliet takes the Friar's potion in Act 4 Scene 3. Imagine what her nightmare would be if the drug did not knock her cold immediately but had hallucinogenic properties. The answer is marrying Paris, of course, on Thursday morning, which are some of the last words of anxiety she expresses before taking the mixture. So we create a scene showing that nightmare – a crazy hen-night party, a dead Tybalt walking through, Paris as the stripper, Romeo trying to reach her but unable to. This short scene is generally considered one of the highlights of the whole production. If extra scenes illuminate something, adding an extra dimension without distorting the play, put them in!

The decision of what to cut from the script was dictated by our awareness of both our young audience and the general paying public. There were two main considerations – that they should see the play *Romeo and Juliet* reasonably intact. Our production ran for two-and-a half hours with the interval. We also felt that a purist approach to keeping in the less accessible scenes, especially in regard to young people, would work against sustaining their interest and enthusiasm.

In my experience, unless you are in a situation where performing a complete script is imperative, it is best not to be precious about scenes or moments that may well be held in high esteem in the English Literature lesson yet take ages to decipher. It is not worth losing your audience, especially first timers to Shakespeare, through being a stickler for the script. For example, several English teachers in the audience expressed their gratitude and gave their blessing to our decision to cut Mercutio's Queen Mab speech in its entirety. Of the individual characters, Mercutio's lines inevitably suffered most in the cuts, along with the Friar's, but whole scenes were cut and replaced with a physical alternative where it was felt to be a stronger way to communicate the story. Sections of every Shakespeare play are hard to connect with and appear anachronistic. How many people can quote or even fully understand the priceless first line of *Romeo and Juliet* uttered by Samson: 'Gregory, o'my word, we'll not carry coals,' without the help of explanatory notes.

At no point is there a cast read-through of the whole play, although as a company we will read a scene together for textual understanding before tackling it. I find this to be a collectively supportive way of giving students the assurance to handle the text, whereas a read-through can have the opposite effect. Both adult and student actors can struggle with reading in a way that bears no relation to their acting skills. If the script is badly read, as it may be at an early stage, then the exercise serves little purpose other than to cause stress. By the whole cast having a go at the same scene in separate small groups, their confidence in approaching the language and playing with it increases significantly. They gain a practical insight into the possibilities and scope for interpretation. Within our company we might end up in one early workshop with eight different versions of the same scene or moment which hopefully embeds the idea that the whole play is open to interpretation and that their own thoughts are as valid as anybody else's. The final production is truly as full of their ideas as of mine.

Out of the several thousand students, some as young as ten, who saw *Romeo and Juliet* in Greenwich and Hammersmith as well as in our own school, thankfully no one offered the feedback we would have been most saddened by: 'I didn't understand what was going on, I didn't understand the language.'

Speaking Shakespearian text poorly and without understanding or emotion is one stereotypical characteristic of the school play. There are few physical impediments that can be blamed – the female parts were all written for young boys, simplified by Shakespeare to take into account their reduced lung capacity (Gibson, 2000). And today's young people are generally a much fitter and healthier bunch than the actors treading the boards of the original Globe. The challenge is to encourage students to speak the language as if they own it, as if this is how they always speak. But technically, they must still be clear, audible, articulate, honouring the rhythms of the verse and able to retain the meaning of a sentence potentially six lines of verse long, by driving the thought through to the end. It is a complex process and takes hours and hours of work. There is no easy shortcut. In exactly the same way you would work with adult actors on classical text, you need students first to discover the exact meaning of the dialogue and how to deliver the verse in a standard, correct, rhetorical fashion and then show the skill and confidence to play with the delivery. Only then can they introduce contemporary cadences, tones and speech patterns into their performance to reflect – in our case – south east London today, while still respecting the inherent stress patterns of Shakespeare's verse, without which the words would make no sense. You as teacher or director need to have absolute confidence with the language yourself and then work to create a culture for students where they realise that, providing the basic rules are obeyed, endless creativity is possible with delivery, just as with any script.

The only way to keep the next generation genuinely interested in Shakespeare when the teaching of it is threatened in schools, is to make it relevant and exciting. It is unfortunate that our school's continued efforts to interest the education departments of the two main Shakespeare producing companies, the Globe and the RSC, in coming to see the production were unsuccessful. Their philosophy of education, I fear, is inherently one way: from their organisations to the schools. There appears to be no genuine interest or belief that there could be anything of worth to them coming the other way. Whilst publicly bemoaning the state of Shakespeare teaching in schools, it is a shame that they miss the opportunity to see examples of good practice. After all, here was a production performed by a school which sold out at Greenwich Theatre, was asked to transfer to Riverside Studios where it also sold out – a play about young people, performed by young people in a style and with a focus that has captivated hundreds of young people in London. You would imagine they might take an interest.

Our production was also a financial success, taking about £20,000 in all at the box-office of the two venues. The cast presented a large proportion of the profit to Damilola Taylor's father, who came to see the show, for the educational work of the Damilola Taylor Trust.

Categorising our work is not straightforward. People write to me after the show and ask me to explain more about our company and I realise that it is not always understood that we are a school production – not a theatre company, nor even youth theatre, but a state secondary school that performs plays to a professional standard. We also happen to be in a borough that is struggling to lift itself off the bottom of the national attainment league tables.

Part of this puzzlement stems from the lack of comparable groups. The closest I have come across are the schools who worked on the plays of Edward Bond and the relationship he had with them. Having never seen those productions, I cannot comment on the standard of acting in the final product. But they are certainly examples of a playwright trusting his material to young people to premiere. Most of the theatre world cannot comprehend what young people are really capable of, as their notion of 'real' theatre does not encompass youth theatre, never mind school theatre. This also includes the drama and education world, who rightly delight in and value the involvement of young people in drama, their connection to 'professional' theatre and the learning that results from that. Historically, they too have shown little respect for young people acting in productions or for the educational benefits and especially the artistic possibilities of what young people can create.

The drama in education community still considers professional theatre as something outside of their own institutions, something done by other people, a product that needs to be bought in if students are to experience it. That is why what we do at Kidbrooke is not mentioned or labelled in academic circles as a movement or an approach. It is simply not considered possible or thought to exist.

From the numerous letters I received from members of the audience at both Greenwich Theatre and Riverside Studios, it is clear that our production of *Romeo and Juliet* not only challenged assumptions about the play and about Shakespeare in general, but also demonstrated that professional standard theatre is not the exclusive preserve of adults, or of certain theatres and organisations, but is achievable by young people in state education, in a school production.

Bibliography/Further Reading

David, D and David, A. (2005) *Edward Bond and the Dramatic Child. Edward Bond's Plays for Young People*. Trentham

Gibson, J.L (2000) *Squeaking Cleopatras: The Elizabethan boy player*. Sutton

Nicholson, H (2009) *Theatre and Education*. Palgrave Macmillan

NASUWT report Gangs and Schools. Telegraph.co.uk 17.04.08

For interviews with Lucy Cuthbertson and members of the cast go to: http://www.youtube.com/watch?v=Cp8wKwEh2fE

Analysing what we and the children are really doing when they play and do drama

'The Play's the Thing...'

Amanda Kipling

Drama is essentially learning though the medium of pretend. Theatre is the communication of what is learned. Drama in Education engages both of these in isolation, and, for the most part, dances in an overlap of the two, making both happen at once.

That is my 'in a nutshell' definition of Drama and Theatre. Teachers have tried long and hard to find a line between the two and most have concluded it is unnecessary – children instinctively know and understand the difference and are fluent in the areas which overlap. All arts depend on an unspoken connoisseurship and students in schools acquire this gift quite naturally. Why is this?

Play – a human birthright

There are certain universal truths: that children play is one. We all learn through playing, as Froebel, Piaget, Bruner and Vygotsky agree. Drama has always enjoyed great popularity at GCSE and A level and examination results are good. Why is this subject so successful? Simply, drama has at its core natural learning through play.

It is no coincidence that the word play is part of words like *player, playhouse, playwright* and so on. Developmentally we have the 'baby puking and mewling' imitating his mother's sounds and facial expressions in play at the start of life. Then we have the plays of Shakespeare, still relevant 400 years on, presenting man engaged in the universal problems of the human condition. In our own way we are all doing the same thing in our nursery play with Wendy houses and toys and *play*mates. Theatre and drama – however one wishes to define them, both and together sit on top of the fundamental universal pattern we all follow: play.

Isn't it just child's play?

This chapter traces the development of play through the early and primary years and offers insights into the implications for secondary drama. I am indebted to Lesley Hendy and Lucy Toon for the way they have tracked the natural developmental stages of play and playing up to what we might term 'drama'. But because their book is entitled *Supporting Drama and Imaginative Play in the Early Years* (2001), secondary teachers might not have come across it.

The current position of play and drama

The arrival of the National Curriculum (1998) and the Literacy (1999) and Numeracy (2000) hours brought about a steady return to whole class teaching throughout primary schools. The Foundation Stage Profile (2003) caused a misfit in terms of continuity and transition: 'learning through play became sidelined. Children's choice of play-based activities was limited to perhaps a tongue in cheek 'golden hour' on a Friday afternoon' (Anning, 2005:19).

And with play went drama. Learning in all areas which had been skillfully accessed through play during the progressive years of the 60s and 70s disappeared in favour of a more deskbound approach.

In 1992 Joan Sallis wrote that

> the greatest danger we face is that our primary schools will lose confidence in the very reforms which have brought visitors from all over the world to see them, and will be afraid to stray from the paths that will lead to the tests. (Sallis, 1992:19)

How true her words have turned out to be.

At present, consciousness of play is high in early years – as might be expected. In Key Stage 1 and Key Stage 2, where dramatic play thrived in accessing challenging issues and exploring the dilemmas of mankind through problem solving and broadening empathetic awareness, all we might now find is some hot-seating in history or random freeze frames. Isolated examples of good practice can still be seen but twenty years after Sallis' comments, teachers skilled in the use of dramatic play are fast disappearing from our classrooms.

Nationally there is a trend for non specialist teachers to have responsibility for drama development at Key Stage 3. The specialists appear as late as Key Stages 4 and 5 – just in time to boost GCSE results for league tables. However, fast track strategies need to be used to gain good results when the foundations are poor. Without the steady, natural organic development which used to permeate teaching and learning, the nature of teaching at this level has changed enormously with spoonfeeding becoming shockingly more and more common.

What about the future?

Early indications from the 2010 Education White Paper do not bode well for play as an important building block for learning or for drama and the arts. Education is an electoral football.

There had been encouraging progress, beginning with *All Our Futures: Creativity, Culture and Education*, the 1999 report to the UK government by the National Advisory Committee on Creative and Cultural Education. The report made clear, as Brian Wolland pointed out, that 'Creative and cultural education are not subjects on the curriculum, they are general functions of education' (Wolland, 2010:xvi).

The *Every Child Matters* Green Paper in 2003 and in its subsequent revisions were humanising additions to the debate on creativity. Prof Alexander's *Cambridge Primary Review* of 2009 reported positively on primary education, endorsing many of the changes that creative teachers had been eager for and paving the way for primary education in the future. After the original National Curriculum was dissolved some scaffolding remained to anchor and stabilise the New Primary National Curriculum, due to start in September 2011.

It recommended sweeping away SATs and the boxed curriculum, favouring instead twelve aims including some familiar echoes from ECM (wellbeing, engagement, empowerment, autonomy, encouraging respect and reciprocity, promoting interdependence, citizenship, celebrating culture, exploring, fostering skills, exciting imagination and enacting dialogue). There would also be eight domains which include broader subject areas such as arts and creativity, language, oracy and literacy, and science and technology. The actual content employed to embrace these aspects is to be left to the school to select. Alexander profiled the opportunity for an integrated curriculum and flagged up the importance of the role of drama, indicating for the first time in many years the pivotal role this subject could play in providing the perfect vehicle for the integrated or semi-integrated curriculum.

In April 2009, Jim Rose carried out a review on behalf of the government. Unusually for such a government report, much of the original spirit of the Cambridge Review was kept and these recommendations were welcomed as the underpinning to the New Primary National Curriculum. Teachers could be released to do what they had long wished to: start teaching in a multilayered fashion, ensuring plenty of contact with the material in as many different ways as possible, with children learning several things at the same time. The laboured, non-efficient boxed curriculum would be left behind.

The vast majority of these primary school teachers had had no experience themselves of an integrated curriculum, so this was certainly not a case of teachers being nostalgic for the good old days. On the contrary, these teachers were arriving at the need for this change through their experience in the classroom, both those in which they had learned and those in which they now taught.

In addition the new curriculum holds that a semi-integrated curriculum should continue into Key Stage 3. This would allow drama to continue to play a core role in teaching and learning right up to the options stage at the end of Key Stage 3.

Teachers are frustrated that the Alexander and Rose reports did not come earlier, so that this new curriculum was established and working before the election. As it is, untried and untested, this long awaited release for learning and opportunity for drama and play to reclaim their rightful profile in learning is a politically vulnerable issue.

Will it make a difference?

Whatever the politicians decide, the pattern of the development of play and its relationship with learning will continue into Key Stage 3 and beyond – no government can change that. Teachers everywhere have been pressing for change and to reverse it would be to court unpopularity – which no party can afford. Experienced and insightful teachers everywhere will continue to do what they have been doing: finding ways of progressing good practice and remaining true to good teaching philosophy, while meeting whatever the inconsistent demands of central government might be in these uncertain political times.

Now is a good time to re-examine play and its role in learning throughout formal compulsory education. We have the hard-fought-for opportunity to establish what can be achieved when the curriculum is appropriately shaped to harness children's natural learning patterns. At last drama has a recognised key role in linking the play from early years through the lost Key Stages 1, 2 and 3 to the GCSE years of Key Stage 4.

Play
The Beginnings

A baby of about five months old, being held by his father, looked at his mother and shook his head at her. She immediately made a laughing face with wide eyes and giant smile and shook her head back. The people around them looked on, smiling. The little interaction went on over several turns until a man close by decided to join in and imitated what the mother had been doing. The baby, instead of responding, looked both puzzled and worried and gazed at the strange man, then back at his mother, then at the man again and so on.

What has this to do with play? I would suggest that the mother and baby have developed a game with rules (your turn/my turn; you do something which I copy; I watch you/you watch me; I am quiet when you do your turn/you are quiet when I do my turn). Each time they enact this turn taking ritual they reinforce the strength of their relationship and the baby builds communicative competence. When a stranger tries to join in this very personal ritual the baby (less than six months old, remember) does not respond but looks to his mother as if to ask 'Who is this person and what right does he have to expect me to respond to him when I have never seen him before?'

Smidt 2010 http://www.tactyc.org.uk/pdfs/Reflection_Smidt.pdf

Sometimes action initiated by Smidt's baby meets matched action; sometimes it provokes a different response. Life is getting complicated and only experience will help sort out the 'what will happen if...?' In this example the baby eventually works out that the game can continue regardless of which adult is playing.

When, however, baby copies daddy who puts the tea cosy on his head when pouring the tea, baby's head disappears into the tea cosy and he cannot see. He cannot match father's behaviour exactly and we laugh. Baby laughs with us. Baby is learning that although there are general patterns and rules, these are likely to break at any time and the result is usually funny. A comic is born – he is laughing at the jokes for the first time, we can see them coming. He goes on to share the same joke with his children.

We need look no further – the basic features of all the favourite and most successful activities in our secondary classrooms are here. Classes will play games like *Simon Says, Follow my Leader* and *Mirror Games* because they are deeply rooted in an innocent past, a time when the game was all that mattered, a time when no one was 'out' and everyone could have a turn if they wanted to. They smile and laugh and focus, as there is nothing to interfere – the space to concentrate on the interaction is there and that is sufficient. When playing games in the lesson the pupils' more complex selves are left behind, all unhelpful clutter has been shed for a while and the group is able to bond unhindered. At this point a class will surprise us as they hold hands, sit back to back, work in mixed pairs and so on. We are safe. Other teachers stand aghast and cannot understand why the students 'don't do that for me'.

Of course this is not for you, it is for them – the children – and this is why drama, which is all about the self, can be harnessed so the most productive self can be brought to the fore, leaving less helpful alter-egos in the wings.

The implications of imitative play for primary and secondary drama classrooms

The games based around imitative play plug directly into a part of the self which was uncluttered and happy and where the game was everything. These games need not remain at Early Years level; they can grow up. Follow my Leader becomes a shadowing or sequencing exercise, and Shoal of Fish involves larger clustered groups where the leader is whoever is at the front, and changes each time the shoal turns by as little as 45 degrees.

Mirror Game becomes more complex as one half of the body leads the partner and the other half mirrors. Copy Cat can be made more complex by the class copying the leader one move behind the sequence. All the vocal warm-ups using repetitive chanting are based on copying and imitative play – even the army uses this technique!

The most familiar improvisation exercise example is the Shadow, where one person is the shadow of another. The result is often quite existentialist as the shadow insists it has no choice – its destiny is to stalk its owner and witness all their doings.

Most secondary lessons require some form of re-cap near the start and imitation activities are a good way of doing this in a productive way. A good example is, 'copy a line and a move from last week – either yours or someone else's'.

Drama lessons which try to start with group improvisation or a continuation of a piece of script work often succumb to distraction and inapporopriate behaviour. Even theatre companies like the Royal Shakespeare Company, Trestle, Frantic Assembly and the National Theatre begin their rehearsals with preparatory exercises – however short – that entail imitative play based activities. Unsurprisingly, they follow with the next stages of play, accessing a deep rooted bank of skills and knowledge, reinforcing the foundations for the on-coming work, clearing the mind of recently acquired clutter and refreshing and re-invigorating the group with shared strengths.

The kinds of play

Psychologists have defined five different kinds of play.

Symbolic play   Everyday objects become 'other' objects

Role play   Being 'another'

Socio-dramatic play   Using child versions of real things to enact social situations

Thematic-fantasy play   Using imagined items and places to explore situations

Play with rules   Games on own or with others

(Hendy and Toon, 2001)

Symbolic play

Moyles (2005:1) offers this description of two young children on safari using an upturned table in the garden.

The boys have no problem whatsoever in using the same item as an imagined other item. They are on safari as themselves, in a different place and in different circumstances.

> Jack (6 years old) and George, (nearly 3 years old) are playing 'safari' in the garden. This consists of mainly chasing visiting cats, stalking various bird inhabitants, speaking in squeak language to a couple of resident squirrels and generally stomping around the garden with magnifiers hunting a range of mini-beasts. They suddenly decide that this imaginative game is worth extending: Jack thinks they need a safari vehicle and George wants a picnic! Together they plan what they need and ask an adult to help them. The partially written and mainly oral lists consists of a tent, compass, a safari vehicle, biscuits, chocolate buttons, jam sandwiches, orange juice and water, a camera, animal books, and paper and felt pens. Having acquired all the small items in self-selected old ice-cream tubs they rush out to the garden again and requisition the upside-down garden table as a vehicle. Somehow however, this does not suit the current mood and the adult is asked if she can think of a way of 'making this (the table) better'. The table is set upright and covered with two old sheets. Suddenly, transformation for the children: the table becomes both vehicle and tent.

In the secondary classroom this capacity is readily recognised at exercise level: passing a pullover around a circle and inviting it to be something else is an old favourite. It takes time so you can extend it by having two jumpers, one going in each direction. This can easily develop into a comedy drama, with the teacher reading a narration (keeping an element of control) and the class in pairs or small groups having to use anything they can find to make the various things they need for the story. Quick thinking, vast imagination, speed – therefore no time for arguing – all ensure the class is working with fun and focus and making new working relationships. Their stronger, less cluttered inner selves aged about four are functioning well aged twelve. They have transformed themselves from a negative group identity into a happy creative one and have thus turned a corner.

At the same time the students are engaging in Brecht's theatre, where the audience has to suspend disbelief and immerse itself in a pretend world where a broom becomes a rifle and a smudge of red paste a war wound and one soldier represents an army. Brecht's style of theatre needed much explanation to the adults of the time. Not so to the children: they had always done it this way.

Role play – being another

The boys on safari were having an adventure not as scientists, not as photographers or film makers but essentially as themselves. They knew they needed a make-believe vehicle but they took real chocolate buttons on their journey.

By Key Stage 4, students are expected to be able to work away from the self – adopt another gender or race, and exist in different time and space contexts. 'This is me going shopping in the nursery corner', eventually becomes, 'I am the ghost of Hamlet's father'. This steady growth away from the self – a fine example of the de-centring stages explored by Piaget (1950) – is complex and highly pertinent to the Early Years classroom. What is sometimes overlooked is that it has significant implications for the secondary classroom too. Looking at role in relation to socio-dramatic play allows us to unpick these stages more deliberately.

Socio-dramatic play

Strictly speaking this involves children using child versions of real things to enact social situations. So in the absence of a pedal car, our two safari explorers employed symbolic play and used a table. We too can be flexible over the realness of the props and instead focus on what is happening in terms of role.

Greta Fine (1984) produced this model to help examine the stages of socio-dramatic play.

Level One Children are in pretend situations as themselves

Level Two Children are in pretend situations as another

Level Three Children are in pretend situations with another

Level Four Children are in pretend situations with another playing both parts

Level One – as themselves

We have seen the young child is most often the self in another situation. Instead of being on safari, the boys might have been playing separately, one imitating someone digging the garden, the other in the pedal car going to the shops. The stretch gets more demanding with the skilled assistance of an adult who explains that the digger has been digging in the wrong place or that the car has gone missing from the car park at the supermarket. A skilled nursery nurse can assist in structuring a dilemma which needs collective resolving. 'What will you do with the big hole you have made?' and 'how are we going to manage without a car?' By entering the play, she is offering a bridge into the further levels which we would recognise as akin to Dorothy Heathcote's 'Man in a Mess' model. There are problems which need solving – and the children have to solve them.

In the secondary classroom the parallel can be clearly seen. After a short burst of imitative play activity, we can move onto activities such as, 'in a space on your own, pack a case – you are leaving. Why are you leaving? How do you feel and how does this make you pack? You have too much, something has to be left behind.' The suitcase is symbolic, the role is the self in another situation – but closely known.

Brian Way held that re-defining the group was an essential process for the start of a drama lesson. We can see that finding a space on your own and tapping into early imitative play in warm ups, fulfils precisely that need.

Writing about Way's work, Gavin Bolton observes:

> The baby discovers and lives most happily in a simple form of isolation until it is about three years old; it then enjoys ... sharing with one other person; then with two others and so on into smaller groups. Integration within a social unit is a sophisticated and later stage of development, very much dependent on full opportunity for experiencing the other stages... (Bolton, 1998:153).

Level Two – as another

The next stage or role is often being mummy or daddy (or being the self doing what mummy and daddy do), imitating the behaviour, opinions and language of these people. Household activities like driving – or planning a journey as in the safari example – are seen in play areas in the nursery. Here we might see daddy kicking the car tyres before a journey, and mummy looking in a cupboard and biting her lip as she realises there's no milk. The beginnings of character work are emerging, and parents squirm as they hear their own words and see their own attitudes presented before them.

In the secondary classroom, Stanislavskian study with the copying of another's behaviour through observation bears close resemblance to this play stage. The last activity progresses to, 'now you are your mother/sister/friend packing – they are leaving for entirely different reasons'. Depending on the context of the group, the stretch, having been prepared in a previous lesson, might be further challenged – it could be Anne Frank packing her case, or a stowaway trying to get onto the Titanic. Both the nursery child and their sixteen year-old intellectual sibling are still alone in their respective drama worlds.

How children being in role as self and as other can be seen in the following example.

A class is in role as a group of town planners who have talked to locals about a proposed road. One reports back as the mouthpiece for the group, unsettled on her chair, pencil in mouth, smiling at her friends, focusing on the work, clearly aware of the 'what if' of the situation but essentially presenting as herself in class.

She is doing what is asked of her – she has listened to the group and is reporting back but she is not in role as a reporter. In contrast, a boy plays the part of a man of 80, clearly immersed in the role, not thinking about what this elderly man might see but empathetically seeing it.

Both he and the girl in the drama could be described as being in role but there is a tangible difference in the distance of the roles. Both are clearly getting what they need from the situation. This is a good example of quality differentiation by outcome, though some drama teachers see it as an unconsidered cop out.

(DES Film (1978) *Early Stages*)

Level Three – with another

So far the drama has been active in the well established basic and known self and known others. Now it has reached the end of the comfort zone, and students are invited to step over that threshold.

In the safari setting one child can see the possibilities of the tent being a vehicle as well, but can he be sure that his co-player can do the same? The imagined world of the individual is to be put to a dramatic test when they enter an imagined world together.

It is in this leap that the drama can often experience difficulties. In the nursery the drama might collapse and rebuild as play is the normal genre of the day for them. 'It's not a car? Okay ...it's a boat!' 'You're not on safari with me? So what are you doing?'...'Okay I will have some tea as well!' (before the chocolate buttons disappear).

A skilled adult might assist this by asking where the vehicle is or how she might get to the other side of the rain forest. Personal observations have provided many examples of how the drama can be resolved in nursery by perhaps becoming a dog, or killing off a character one does not wish to play or have in the drama. The player resurrects herself and becomes another and the play continues. On safari one can become the lion and then, once slain, can return as the other's safari co-partner. We see the multi-role begin to emerge. Cohen and Cohen give this example

> Simon pretends to be a captain on a boat ...To attract attention he yells, 'I'm a dead captain – I've got an arrow in there,' pulling up his vest and poking his tummy. 'Let's take the arrow out,' says Christopher. 'Let's leave him till he gets better,' says Mark. However Simon does not like being left alone and announces he is a shark.
>
> (Cohen and Cohen, 1988:184)

For the young there are all kinds of ways of getting into and out of situations. Later on however, embarrassment might set in after one or two failed attempts, as adolescent self-consciousness over the play going wrong can override developments at this vulnerable stage. Drama teachers instinctively place safety nets on the situation: keeping girls as girls, altering the period of the action from the present to the time of their mothers, offering stepping stones for them to use if needed. The teacher might keep the class in role as students of their own age but take them back a hundred years and use teacher in role to maintain the drama impetus by presenting a new angle which can invite a new direction to a slipping drama.

Others will recognise that they support this delicate transition by using pictures and copying them into freeze frames to appropriate music. They might use visualisation, they might set some research and have imaginative ways of accessing small details from this to form the basis of a meditation type journey into the context. (Again we see Stanislavsky's patterns as the sixth form bring in an object the character might posses.) Essentially this is the same bridge we all had to negotiate years ago in the early years.

Level Four – with another playing both parts

This is the most complex and interesting of stages to observe. If our nursery child is suggesting going to rescue the trapped baby tiger and his friend carries on playing with his car, you might see the parent imitation in action. 'You can drive the car afterwards, this tiger is important.' This may be followed by in role direction, 'come on, hold my hand and we'll go together,' which might be taken up or rejected. Children will know when the response, 'I don't want to rescue a tiger. I want to play with the car,' is in role – whether it is provoking a drama conflict or a real desire to play bricks and not pretend safari rescue.

Sometimes a friend does not know how to join in with the proposed drama and here you will witness a vast array of perceptions and languages being employed at the same time. Take Fleming's example of two children playing doctors. Intermittently a child

> ...steps outside the drama to direct the action. 'Then you tell the little boy ... then you be the little boy ... tomorrow you are very, very poorly ... then you phone up...' Despite being completely absorbed in the activity there is a full awareness throughout that this is a fiction, being consciously crafted by the participants. (Fleming, 1998:81)

Secondary and primary teachers alike will recognise that this is the stuff that group improvisations are made of. Here the students are providing bridges for each other by offering their own views, metaphors, even providing models to copy in order to keep the group in the shared imagined environment and make sure no one slips away from it. Once this stage is reached, they have assumed the role the teacher was playing in the previous stage as drama rescuer/reinforcer and doing it themselves. The class can manage the complex group dynamics which are both pressurising and easing, feeding and starving, resolving and complicating the drama which now resembles a microcosm of man's dilemma. We have now reached the stage which is recognised as ripe for Dorothy Heathcote's 'Man in a Mess' being explored together. Heathcote used Kenneth Tynan's definition of drama to arrive at this model.

> Good drama ... is made up of the thoughts, the words, the gestures that are wrung from human beings on their way to, or in, or emerging from a state of desperation. (Extracted by Heathcote from Tynan, 1973)

Young nursery dramatists do not shy away from death and suffering. If the teacher goes into role she may join them and work from within, feeding support and challenge as required, or, as Heathcote was known to do, stand back and let them resolve the drama's dilemmas for themselves.

We move towards her famous Mantle of the Expert model, simply but beautifully captured in the BBC Omnibus documentary *Three Looms Waiting* (1971). Here we see a child with special needs slide in and out of role with ease as he pulls his teaching assistant away from the 'fire' to reassure him: 'they were only pretend matches.' He is deeply involved in the drama, but worries in case his assistant fears that he might be really burnt. He can be involved in role at the same time as appreciating that another might not be coping. He designs strategies to deal with that, and then returns to the drama. Within seconds he demonstrates all four levels of socio-dramatic play.

Thematic fantasy play

This occurs when a child essentially mimes the world he exists in. The development is similar and in many respects can go alongside the socio-dramatic play model, though usually realism is what we see first in the nursery, with fantasy and magic coming later when stories and films have had a chance to make an impact. Consequently the need for toy kitchens and cars begins to disappear, replaced by mimed, imagined people, monsters, spaceships and so on.

The following model enables us to recognise some of the examples already given and again to realise consciously exactly what we are doing when we design a lesson that goes well. The direct connections are evident in the context of what has been outlined before in socio-dramatic play. We can superimpose the next layer on socio-dramatic play as here we have the development of what might be seen as more akin to theatre.

Smilansky and Shefatya (1990) offer a developmental model

Imitative role play	Child assumes a make-believe role and uses imitative action/verbalisation
Make believe with regard to toys	Toys and materials are moved around as characters/ 'other' things

Verbal make believe with regard to actions or situations	Narration substitutes action and situation
Persistence in role play	Maintains role play developmentally for at least ten minutes
Interaction	At least two children play together within the context of the story
Verbal communication	There is dialogue related to the play

Imitative role play

Here comes the imaginative use of language, such as the squeak language, our intrepid heroes used while on safari. With it comes stylised movement – the stealthy creeping up on the animals and taking of photographs. The other supports this by wincing as a footstep is heard or signalling with exaggerated silent panic when a tiger is seen. In the secondary drama classroom we recognise this as the fabric of mime skills. While we might not teach mime separately, we do progress its use. Moving from making a cup of tea to being thrown across the room by a bomb blast are similarly rooted in this essential play skill.

Make believe with regard to toys

We saw earlier how the jumpers were used in a warm-up game and confidence continues to grow as secondary students use lengths of fabric to represent a myriad of things and feelings, such as white silk for a shroud, red net as rage. We take them to see productions like the National Theatre's *A Caucasian Chalk Circle* (1997), where broom handles created the famous broken bridge and also the flowing river.

Verbal make believe with regard to actions or situations

During the process of drama, directions will be given to others. 'Go on, get into the ambulance then!' 'No! Not like that, limp, like this....'

In addition, gobble-de-gook and made-up names for people (Mr Smelly Pots the plumber, for example) abound in the nursery and we have to think about how this translates in our secondary classrooms. It does happen when students are in role as someone far from the self and they use words they have heard but may not understand, or words they have not heard before, when depth of role forces the language out from an unknown somewhere.

Persistence in role play

The children on safari modelled persistence over two hours. If another is involved, there are more opportunities for the child to explore relationships, issues of gender, status, identities and problem solving. Input can be equal. If alone, exploration is possible but play runs the risk of the safari remaining at the level of chasing next door's cat.

At secondary level we see the foundations of the requirements for GCSE as groups devise work that ensures equal exposure for each candidate and the evolution of democratic ensemble work.

Interaction and verbal communication

Children are using language in possibly more varied modes than their own or that of their parents and teachers, maybe utilising hero language from TV or villain language from stories. The repertoire is opening up choices and the skills required for exploring text work, such as about the ghost of Hamlet's father, are now in place.

We are familiar with certain recurring broad features of role:

> *Action* – driving a car, making a drink, going shopping and so on. The human quality does not matter – the action is what is of importance.

> *Stereotypical character* – the teacher, the policeman, the old lady etc. Their task or mission is what is important.

> *Fictional character* – the super hero, big bad wolf, the prince, the giant, the fairy and so on. Their character, personality, values, philosophy take on importance.

Morgan and Saxton (1987) offer a more detailed model, designed to help teachers categorise the various ways in which children enter the drama.

Dramatic playing	As self in make believe situation
Mantle of the Expert	As self but with special eyes
Role playing	In role representing an attitude or point of view
Characterising	Representing an individual lifestyle, somewhat different from child's own
Acting	Selecting symbols, movements, gestures, and voices to represent a particular individual to others. (Presenting or performing)

The first four examples are familiar and we can see how when these stages have been worked through, skills seen as theatrical become available to the pupils. Indeed some are already in use.

Games with rules

We tend to avoid these in schools as they are competitive and bring out differences among the students which we are trying to work against. They often involve players being 'out', letting the accumulating rejected children grow in antagonism in the corner while the teacher carries on with the winners. By the time the teacher is ready to start the first drama activity, a resentful pack of disinterested students has formed. Their negative selves have returned and festered while the rest have been playing. Consequently, games need to be used with care or adapted to bring about the success we associate with the imitative play games described.

Take, for example, Grandmother's Footsteps, which can be played slowly, with dressing up options as Trestle Theatre do as an exercise, so the focus is not on winning but on interacting increasingly creatively with the others.

What might we take into secondary from the primary play models?

Secondary practitioners can see how shaping the first fifteen minutes of a lesson, selecting elements of all the above in an appropriate order, can lead us to the openings we need to achieve depth and creativity in our lessons. These stages need not be followed slavishly, but the lesson plan should be evaluated for how well it follows these stages with classes we find challenging. If the first ten minutes of a lesson go well the rest is likely to do so too. We acquire insight into what works and why our fail safe lessons might be so successful.

We can see what the early practitioners' words of wisdom mean for us. A basic formula could look like this:

- a game/activity based on imitation with an element of re-cap
- find a space on your own – in role as yourself
- now as another – moving the self a little further away
- now in a pair – now sharing that otherness with another
- now teacher provides a story/situation and the structure replays swiftly and fluently into the secondary school drama lesson: the whole class is immersed in the drama and another world exists

Each element can be so disguised that it can take many years of secondary experience to spot this as a formula. Its variations are endless – in a sense it is not a formula at all. If we believe that play is the basis of drama and is innate, it makes sense to use something along these lines to assist planning.

This explains why drama lessons which consisted of 'get into groups and do a play about...' fell flat. Similarly any lesson starting in groups is likely to falter, likewise anything starting with 'come on, you remember where we were last week. Stop fighting and get into role,' or anything starting with dialogue. In life, our ability to communicate verbally comes after much other learning, so it makes sense for dialogue to come later in the lesson, even if only ten minutes later.

...over-teaching what they know already
I leave you with a poignant story.

A group of PGCE Secondary Drama students spent a day with Jo Somervell, a primary drama specialist and leader of the Barking and Dagenham School Centred Initial Training (SCITT) team. In the afternoon she taught a primary class. When telling the story of the minotaur, she touched the children on the shoulder and they got up and instantly became the trees, the minotaur, the king, the queen and so on. They instinctively acted out what was required. She never had to explain what a still image was, neither did she have to ask them. The lesson went on in the same vein when she went into role – they joined in with no need to labour what teacher-in-role meant. The lesson was seamless, rich and challenging. With no hesitation, they engaged and worked with diligence.

A student leaned over to me and whispered, 'I have just realised how much time we waste in secondary schools over-teaching students what they know already.'

References
Alexander, R (ed) (2009) *Children, their World, their Education: final report and recommendations of the Cambridge Primary Review.* Routledge

Anning, A (2005) Play and legislated curriculum: back to basics? In Moyles, J (ed) *The Excellence of Play.* Open University Press

Bolton, G (1998) *Acting in Classroom Drama.* Trentham Books

Bruce T (2004) *Developing Learning in early Childhood.* Paul Chapman

Cohen, A and L (1988) *Early Education: the pre-school years.* Paul Chapman

DES Film (1978) *Early Stages*

Fleming, M (1998) *Starting Drama Teaching.* David Fulton

Heathcote, D (1973) *Three Looms Waiting.* BBC TV Documentary

Hendy, L and Toon, L (2001) *Supporting Drama and Imaginative Play in the Early Years.* Open University Press

Morgan, N and Saxton, J (1987) *Teaching Drama: a mind of many wonders.* Heinemann

Rose, J (ed) (2009) *Independent Review of the Primary Curriculum: final report.* DfE Publications

Sallis, J (1992) In Black, P (ed) (1992) *Education: Putting the Record Straight.* Network Educational Press

Smidt S (2009) The play's the thing: redefining and rethinking play http://www.tactyc.org.uk/pdfs/Reflection_Smidt.pdf

Smilansky, S and Shefatya, L (1990) *Facilitating Play: a medium for cognitive, socio-emotional and academic achievement in young children.* Bartleby Press

Somers. J (1994) *Drama in the Curriculum.* Cassell

Woolland, B (2010) *Teaching Primary Drama.* Longman

Making the 14-19 Creative and Media Diploma work

Guerrillas in the studio
Training interventions and blended professionalism in the delivery of the 14-19 Creative and Media Diploma
Emma Brown

The Tomlinson Report, *14-19 Curriculum and Qualifications Reform* (2004) highlighted four main concerns:

- at the top end of the ability range British teenagers are very accomplished
- the bottom 40 per cent are being failed by the present system
- 300,000 leave school with no qualifications
- fewer than 50 per cent gain Grade C or better in GCSE Maths and only 56 per cent in English

In proposing reform, Tomlinson suggested that:

- all 14 to 19 year olds should leave secondary school with a graduation certificate or diploma
- a newly developed diploma should be introduced with four levels: entry, foundation, intermediate and advanced
- vocational experience and qualifications will score towards a diploma as well as GCSEs and A levels
- participation in special vocational or academic projects and community service will also add points
- international models add research weight to the suggested reform agenda

n 2005 the Government responded by publishing the White Paper 14-19 *Education and Skills,* setting out their plans for wholesale reform of the 14-19 Curriculum. Underpinning these reforms was strategic concern over the traditional distinction between vocational (Unwin, 2009) and academic learning. In 2004, the Learning and Skills Research Council had offered the following definition:

> Those experiences and activities that lead to (or aim to lead to) outcomes (either) in the form of vocational qualifications or where the learning is not certificated, ... clearly linked with developing an individual's competence in his/her current occupational area. (LSRC, 2004:2)

The 2005 white paper (see Appendix 1 for a summary) offered a mixed bag of revision and reform, setting out a statutory requirement upon schools and colleges to collaborate. However, Government amendments to some of the most radical elements of Tomlinson's report angered many people. The slippage between policy and practice offered a particularly paradoxical environment for curriculum designers operating at local level. Between 2005 and the 2008 launch date, 14-19 learning providers were asked to design curriculum models which embraced the four 'suites of learning'. These were Diplomas, Apprenticeships, Foundation Learning and alternative traditional qualifications such as A levels and BTECs. The aim was to create a system of qualifications that would provide a choice of routes leading to valuable qualifications in themselves and progression to further learning.

By organising themselves into local consortia and preparing 'gateway' bids for delivery of the new Diplomas, teachers were embracing a new 'practitioner' identity, one which concerns facilitation rather than delivery and seeks to position the learner at the heart of a project-based pedagogic model.

Integral to this model is the concept of work-related learning defined by the Department for Children, Families and Schools as 'planned activity which uses the context of work to develop skills, knowledge and understanding which will be useful in working life.' Since all Diploma learners must undertake at least ten days of work related learning and the logistics of this appeared daunting, a range of alternative approaches were mooted, including employer visits to schools or colleges and mentoring. At least half of the 'principal learning' component of each Diploma is intended to be 'applied'. In the context of work-related learning, this refers to the process of acquiring and developing knowledge, skills and understanding through tasks set in sector contexts that have many of the characteristics of real work, or tasks that are set within the workplace.

> Every young person should experience the world beyond their classroom. These experiences change lives. (Alan Johnson, Education Secretary, 2006)

A composite qualification offered at three (sequential levels): Foundation, Higher and Advanced, the three components of the Diploma are as follows:

- Principal Learning – the subject specific element of the qualification
- Generic Learning – Functional Skills and Personal Learning and thinking Skills – mandatory for all learners
- Work – Related Learning

In their professional development programme for consortia developed during the 2008/09 academic year, the Specialist Schools and Academies Trust (SSAT) asked delegates to consider the concept of employability. In the context of a contemporary global 'experience economy' (Pine and Gilmore, 1999), and recent rises in unemployment levels, it is clearly essential that young people are well equipped to encounter industrial workplaces. A robust Information and Guidance Strategy (IAG) is therefore deemed of huge importance and this was statutorily enshrined in the 2009 white paper.

The problematic emphasis on practitioner agency as a key driver of the reform agenda was recently highlighted by Lorna Unwin, whose description of the Diploma as the 'latest in a long line of government-led initiatives over the past 20 years that might be classed as a vocational tease' helps to remove us further from an analysis of the qualification as a post-modern qualification:

> The Diplomas area form of obese cuckoo in the education nest, stuffed full of academic requirements which will work hard to push out the more expensive and complex vocational component. The cuckoo may well fly, largely due to the hard work of teachers in schools and colleges, supportive employers and willing students. But its chances of survival would be far greater if it were allowed to concentrate on developing its vocational identity. (Unwin, 2009:3)

Landscape of interaction(s)

Amongst the wealth of materials commissioned and published by a range of government agencies and quangos, the Learning and Skills Improvement Agency (LSIS) have arguably been the most prolific. To support the launch of the first phase of diplomas, in 2008 LSIS published a *Practitioner Guide to the Diploma*. In a section focused on 'managing and supporting partnership working', the guide describes the 'implications of collaborative working for practitioners':

> To ensure that learners are receiving specialist skills delivery, consortia are carrying out skills and training needs analysis of staff ... as staff leave or are promoted into different roles, an opportunity arises to address gaps in the delivery of the Diploma across the consortium and to fill them with the best match. This means that teaching contracts will also begin to change: many will now include the requirement to travel to a number of sites within an authority to deliver a specialism. While this workforce development is in progress, consortia will rely on their links with employers and schools, colleges and universities to ensure that the requirement for delivery by a specialist is being met. (LSIS, 2008:101)

The range of possible stakeholders listed here gives some indication of the expectation of the deployment of advanced communication skills. In a landscape characterised by 'relational complexity' (Barnett, in Cunningham, 2008), the Diploma Practitioner is thus asked to use his or her 'situated knowledge' (Friedson, 2001:25) and through the mediated reality of a range of practical interactions (with learners and colleagues) also rely on a further level of what Eraut calls 'tacit knowledge':

> We may assume that some of [that] practical knowledge and skill is tacit, and therefore neither verbalised nor codified. Tacit knowledge of the concrete circumstances in which virtually any kind of work must be performed is as essential to performance as the skills employed to use it. (Freidson, 2001:31)

Since the vocational experience of being on the job is neither spatially demarcated nor socially situated, the Diploma Practitioner's knowledge base, its curriculum and pedagogic frameworks, may be said to acquire a reified status. Concepts such as 'employer engagement' and 'facilitated learning' become part of the language of the new space. Halpin's (2005:6) search for a 'new meta-language for understanding the complex relations prevailing between changes taking place in the broader social formation and adjustments concurrently underway at the micro-institutional level of personal and professional identity' resonates strongly here as the practitioner is asked to traverse the complex territory of 'change management', employing the leadership skills of diplomacy, advocacy and logistical visioning to ensure that partnership planning and implementation has a strong strategic direction. The Diploma Practitioner guide provides the following illuminating 'reflective checklist for partnership working':

- ■ are you prepared to *trust* colleagues from other institutions?
- ■ can you respect others and the contributions they make?
- ■ can you accept a majority decision that conflicts with your own wishes?

- are you *flexible yet focused*?
- are you prepared to act as an ambassador for collaboration?
- can you remain *positive* when problems arise?
- do you want to be part of a successful partnership?

(2008:103)

It is to the common spaces created by the diploma lines of learning to which we now turn, in order to examine the characteristics of these newly created, democratic, communities of practice (Lave and Wenger, 1991).

The Creative and Media Diploma

The **Creative and Media Diploma** (CMD) was one of the first five Diplomas to be launched in September 2008 and to date has the highest number of registered learners and the largest numbers of active consortia. It is offered at all three Diploma levels by the three major awarding bodies: AQA, OCR and Edexcel.

The creative and cultural sector is a notoriously volatile employment environment characterised by large numbers of freelance portfolio workers and small to medium sized enterprises (SMEs). In September 2008 Skillset, the Sector Skills Council (SSC) for Creative Media, developed a local market intelligence document intended for use by those involved in the Skillset footprint – namely TV, Radio, Film Animation, Computer Games, Interactive Media etc. This was followed by a parallel document published by Creative and Cultural Skills (CCS), the SSC for the creative and cultural industries and covering the following sub-sectors: Advertising, Craft, Cultural Heritage, Design, Literature, Music, Performing Arts and Visual Arts. The key statistics set out in these documents make interesting reading and are summarised below:

- total employment across the Creative and Cultural Industries (CCI) in 2008 was 678,480, the Creative Media industry accounts for 537,100 people; employment in these industries increased by 9 per cent between 2006 and 2008
- the CI as a whole contribute 7.3 per cent of the UK's Gross Domestic Product
- export services totalled £14.6billion in 2005
- over one third of the CI works in London and half in London and the South East
- the CI utilise a highly qualified workforce – over half are graduates (56%)
- the CI workforce has 42 per cent of women compared with 46 per cent in the labour market overall, and is a predominantly young working population with 54 per cent under 40

- around one third of the Creative Media workforce earns less than £20,000 per annum and half between £20,000 and £50,000; 41 per cent are self- employed
- there are 74,640 businesses in the CI, 87 per cent of them employ less than ten people

www.skillset.org.uk; www.ccs.org.uk

In such a rapidly changing, complex landscape, it is crucial for teachers of Drama and Performing Arts that material which is developed to inform young people of the key features of the new Diploma stresses the range of career options open to them as a result of studying across so many varied disciplines, as well as the potential strengths and weaknesses of a career in the creative industries. The National Education Business Partnership Network is the umbrella organisation and national voice for the126 Education Business Partnerships (EBPs) working across eleven regions and has key responsibility for helping schools and colleges design and disseminate appropriate material to inform the range of stakeholders (students, parents, colleagues and governors) of the context of the Diploma and its many benefits. EBPs are also remitted to assist in the auditing of the local creative and cultural infrastructure in order to ascertain which businesses might be interested in forging partnerships to help develop the Diploma.

Consortia planning requires line leads (each Diploma line of learning should assign a lead, based within one of the schools or colleges but remitted to facilitate consortia planning for the specific Diploma for which they have responsibility) to engage with the design and implantation of a consortia – wide strategy for both principal and generic learning . All new awarding body specifications for GCSE (new specifications from September 2009) and AS and A2 contain detailed information about both these core elements of their course design. There is also detailed guidance on the plotting of Functional Skills (FS) across the Key Stage 3 curriculum requiring every secondary school to ensure that departments have their own strategy for addressing this issue. Interestingly, although ICT and Numeracy may appear to present more of a challenge than Literacy, a skills shortage in technical theatre presents an excellent opportunity for young people who express interest in this particular area to gain experience of applying their functional skills in the service of the technical theatre crew or production team.

Planning Models

The Diploma is configured over three specific levels, which can be summarised as follows:

- **Level 1** The purpose of the Creative and Media principal learning at level 1 is to provide a basic **introduction** to a range of creative and media sectors, in terms of knowledge of the industry and practical skills central to a range of disciplines. Learners will benefit from an insight into the creative and media industries and the skills required to pursue further study in the line of learning at level 2: **Foundation Diploma**

- **Level 2** The purpose of the Diploma in Creative and Media at level 2 is to encourage learners to further **explore** a range of practical skills, and to develop a broad underpinning knowledge. This qualification will provide the tools with which to explore creative ideas, and to develop them from an increasingly informed perspective: **Higher Diploma**

- **Level 3** The purpose of the level 3 Diploma is to encourage sophistication of thought and application, as well as a higher degree of critical appraisal. Learners are encouraged to **develop** the intellectual and practical skills which will meet higher education entry requirements, as well as the transferable skills and knowledge that support other progression routes: **Advanced Diploma**

In addition, the generic content of the principal learning is structured in to four Themes:

- T1 Creativity in Context
- T2 Thinking and Working Creatively
- T3 Principles, Processes and Practice
- T4 Creative Businesses and Enterprise

The scale and extent of change of the Diploma agenda means that curriculum planning is complex, although QCDA are keen to stress the holistic design of the qualification. The CCS declared its vision:

> The Diploma in Creative and Media offers a chance for employers to engage with young people as creators, participants, receivers and consumers of cultural life. It provides a unique opportunity for organisations to influence the kind of learning that young people experience; to ensure that they are developing the knowledge, skills and behaviour that will benefit the sector. (www.ccskills.org.uk)

Close collaboration with consortia partners and local employers is essential once the choice of awarding body and specification has been made. Schemes of work which can be mapped across schools and colleges and which involve site-specific learning or response to a live brief provided by an employer will be more pragmatically realised if all parties are equally involved at the planning stage. Drama teachers used to working with theatre companies or specialist workshop leaders should have expertise in this area, although a multidisciplinary scheme of work may require some inter-arts collaboration which is less familiar. Imagine schemes of work which take participants to new places, where the pedagogic principles of facilitation present the teacher with new challenges to their identity and the student with new roles in their own learning.

> Work experience is an important component of the Diploma; however, the scope of employer engagement with education generally is far broader and far more meaningful, beneficial and sustainable. It refers to direct employer and industry practitioner involvement with education, learning and development. In relation to the Diploma, it describes a level of involvement that is intrinsic to the ethos of the Diploma and essential to its successful delivery. (www.Skillset. org.uk)

Organising the work-related learning aspects of the Diploma can be a challenging task for consortia faced with possible competition from other local consortia for limited numbers of organisations with sufficient capacity to service the needs of the area or even region. Large employers who have signed up to work with consortia on delivery of the Diploma are known to both EBPs and regional Support Partners (employed directly by SSAT in order to facilitate implementation of the Diploma across consortia in a specific region). They variously include theatres, media organisations, design companies (including fashion, graphic design and advertising) and galleries. Strategic organisations including Arts Council England (ACE) and the Museums, Libraries and Archives Council (MLAC) also have regional development officers, who are remitted to support schools and colleges as they seek to broker appropriate and sustainable partnerships.

Work related learning can take a number of forms, including the following. All of which can be negotiated as part of the consortia's employment engagement strategy:

- using live project briefs, technical specifications etc
- theatre company in residence
- interviewing employees to explore job roles
- attending local steering groups/forums

Skillset has published industry specific guidance in this area and has dedicated a section of the website to setting out case studies, examining emerging relationships between consortia and cultural sector organisations (www.skillset.org/uploads/pdf/asset). DCSF have also published a Work-related Learning Guide aimed 'at everyone involved in work-related learning – young people and their parents, carers, employers, schools and colleges' (www.dcsf.gov.uk/14-19/documents/work-relatedlearningguide).

In the regions, local organisations associated with training and development for the sector have also developed resources and involved themselves in partnership building, in London, see for example the excellent LONSAS website www.lonsas.org,uk and in the West Midlands www.aliss.org.uk, www.Musicleader.net also has resources for the music education community and links to Theatre and Dance resources.

One of the most useful pedagogic models of knowledge transfer between practitioners in education and cultural sector is the project. Since projects provide the dominant paradigm for industry professionals working to commissions or specific briefs, it is important that diploma practitioners understand the cyclical nature of the process and seek ways to simulate it within schemes of work and project briefs. A great deal of work has been done in this area by the awarding bodies whose CPD offer for new Diploma teachers is extensive.

Planning the project

The project is a specific element of the Diploma which is integrated within all three levels and mandatory within the assessment scheme ratified by QCA. It 'allows learners to demonstrate the planning, research and presentation skills required by employers and universities,' and at Advanced level, the project is a stand-alone qualification. The project 'can provide students with a different style of learning from the one they would usually experience. Work can take place in different settings – for example work experience or events run by a university or other organisation, adding variety to learning' (*Guidance on managing Project Delivery*, www.qcda.org,uk).

Each project has to be personalised to the learner, a focus negotiated and a facilitator nominated to help tutor and monitor progress. The mentor or tutor can also be an industry professional. The chosen topic must be confirmed by the consortia centre as relevant to the principal learning, complimenting themes highlighted in the schemes of work and supporting learner progression. Awarding body assessment objectives emphasise the process of developing the project beyond the final course outcome, although a success-ful realisation is directly linked to the quality of the process. Projects might be evidenced in a wide variety of formats including journals, slides, DVDs, CDs, photographs and other artefacts. This non-traditional form of assessment needs careful collaborative planning if learners are to be robustly supported. Learners clearly need to be supported by project skills workshops (which can also be linked to the delivery of functional skills) and this provision can be offered as an extra-curricular activity, perhaps in the form of a participation in an established scheme like the Arts Award. The process of working through the project is illustrated in the following diagram:

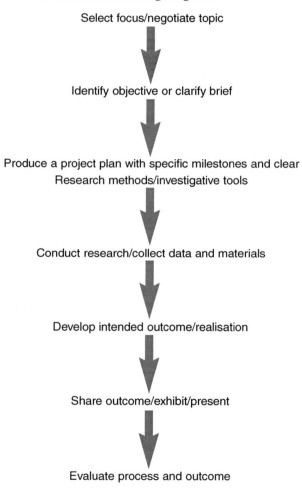

Select focus/negotiate topic

Identify objective or clarify brief

Produce a project plan with specific milestones and clear
Research methods/investigative tools

Conduct research/collect data and materials

Develop intended outcome/realisation

Share outcome/exhibit/present

Evaluate process and outcome

The drama teacher could thus be a facilitator both of arts-based students potentially working across subject areas and also of non-arts students looking to explore elements of the Creative and Cultural Sector as it overlaps with their chosen area of study, eg an engineering student looking at lighting rigs for pop concerts.

Case Studies
1. Knowsley Consortia, Cheshire

Knowsley Collegiate 11-18 Consortia was successful in its bid to become one of the first to deliver the Creative and Media Diploma from September 2008. Their design and implementation of the Diploma have since proved to be exemplary, with approximately 60 learners registered on Level 2 in the 08-09 academic year. The consortia consist of four partners: three schools and a college and the Diploma is offered both at Level 2 and Level 3 using project

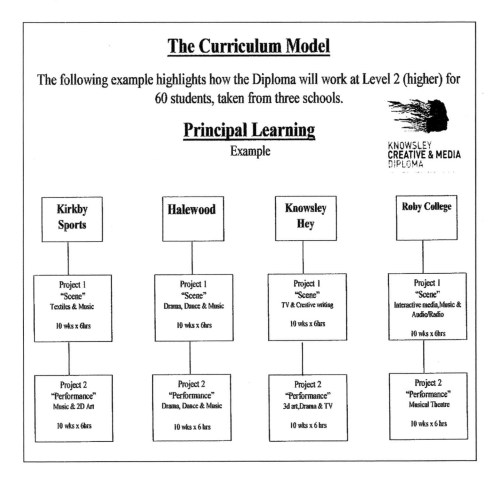

based Schemes of Work which use the titles of units drawn from their choice of Diploma specification. Key to their success is the emphasis on collaboration with all partners. Offering three Diploma Lines – Engineering, Creative and Media and ICT – the consortia appointed a 14-19 Diploma Co-ordinator and Lead practitioners for each line of learning. These practitioners meet monthly and also facilitate monthly network meetings creating a forum for Diploma practitioners and employers to discuss issues arising and find mutually supportive solutions. A clear through-line strategy for delivery maps Key Stage 2 planning (reference to feeder schools) to a hybrid creative enterprise Key Stage 3 curriculum, a14-19 strategy, planning for promoting Higher Education and a strategy for employer engagement.

Whilst each partner retains their own choice of disciplines, the seven units are planned in common across the consortia. At each level a minimum of two staff are required to deliver across the disciplines, and despite the difficulties in managing the logistics of delivery, the consortia eventually settled on dedicated Diploma days, with delivery of the principal learning taking place at the same time each week at all levels, with extended curriculum time designated for delivery of the project. Using real briefs and employers acting as consultants help shape both individual projects and consortia Schemes of Work. The planning has been extensive but worthwhile. Emphasis on co-construction of learning has specific implications for the importance of IAG, as potential Diploma learners need to understand the degree of ownership which is required of them. Klare Murray, lead practitioner for Knowsley, explains the strategy as follows:

> In order to determine who the Diploma is best suited to, it has been important to view it as a unique educational programme that is neither vocational nor academic. The level of rigour, however, has led us to create a series of criteria which will enable us to identify a suitable initial cohort:
>
> ■ passion for the sector, as evidenced by commitment to extra curricular and activities outside of school
> ■ learners that already display some level of PLTS development i.e. independence, initiative, creativity and ability to manage own time.
> ■ attendance
> ■ attitude
> ■ minimum Level 5 in English and Maths
> ■ minimum Level 5 in relevant subject i.e. Creative Arts based subjects
>
> www.artslearningconsortium.org.uk/alcevents

In addition, employer engagement began with an audit of local employers. This was made possible through two informal seminars involving about 25 employers. Five or six large organisations were then identified, including Bluecoat Arts Centre, and local theatres with representatives in attendance at planning days and the development of an Events Matrix where students could have direct access to specific workplaces. Although this has been a complex and demanding operation, the Diploma has clearly been highly valued. Asked to comment on the first year of delivery, Klare Murray identifies the following key messages:

▦ Consider Assessment roles and responsibilities. In Knowsley we have shaped our assessment and moderation process to mirror our Quality Assurance Framework. First the portfolio is assessed by the individual practitioners within the institution where the learner studied. Then the network meet and all portfolio marks are agreed across institutions. The assessment grades are then quality assured at the Lead Practitioner and Partnership level.

▦ The Diploma is a composite qualification, you must insure when reporting to parents that this is clearly explained. In Knowsley we are sending home an end of Unit Report with a unit mark and effort grade, with a header to parents indicating that principal learning is only one aspect of the overall Diploma. In July we will send out an End of Year Diploma Report including ASL, Project, Functional Skills, PLTS and Principal Learning units covered so far.

▦ Ensure you are involving your exams officers at all stages, they need to be aware where all learners are studying for each unit so they can register them to the correct assessment centre.

2. West Somerset Consortia

In September 2008 the Somerset Consortia launched the Creative and Media Diploma with students enrolled at all three levels and with reference to the AQA specification. With a similar model to the one outlined in the first case study, four partners started to plan across a range of disciplines. One day was agreed for the delivery of principal learning and another for delivery of additional and specialist learning and the Extended Project. The following diagram exemplifies this model (see page 126).

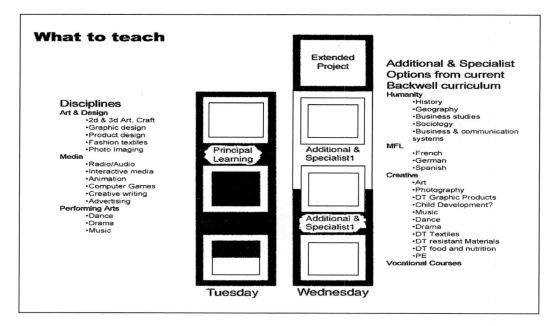

Creative Industries Audit

Using a six projects model to deliver across the academic year, partners worked together to ensure that delivery simulated the ways of working of industry.

For lead practitioner Mark Curtis, the most important decision was about creating 'the appropriate project for each delivering institution tailored to meet the strengths of the institution and intake using the common project based consortium model, and the consortia project criteria. We can also consider which disciplines could be taught, driven from the needs of the project'. In the rural landscape of Somerset, consortia have faced a different set of challenges with fewer regularly funded organisations to work with, and greater distances between workplaces and, indeed, consortia institutions. Although funding for Diploma start up and delivery has hitherto been directed through local authorities, allocation of resources to specific centres is at the discretion of the consortia. Numbers of registered learners, resource levels, transport needs, are all factors requiring considerable thought. In North Somerset, the applied magazine project has seen the consortia partner with local newspaper journalists and graphic design agencies.[1]

Mark Curtis has the final word:

> I was quite cynical about the Diploma when I first heard about it, say 18 months
> ago or so. I thought somebody else was going to be teaching my students, and

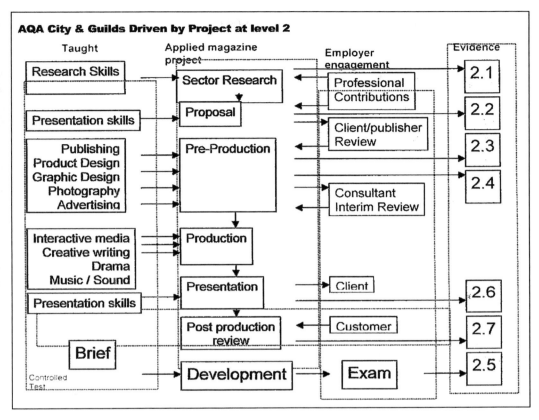

AQA City & Guilds Driven by Project at level 2

that's the way I thought about it, but I'm completely sold on the premise now. It's a very real experience and the students get a lot from it. They're punching well above their weight and that's as a result of the style of delivery.

3. Ricards Lodge School, Wimbledon

Sarah Sawyer, Director of Specialism at Ricards Lodge, conceived a scheme of work to engage her students in the background and events leading up to The First World War and the use of working horses in the battlefields. The scheme of work was designed to engage Key Stage 4 students specifically in the study of the National Theatre's critically acclaimed production of Michael Morpurgo's *War Horse*. She worked with Rachel Lillywhite from The Engine Room to frame the project as a pilot for the new Creative and Media Diploma to be taught in some Merton Schools from September 2009 and at Ricards Lodge from September 2010. The project was designed to test methods of delivery and partnership models for the new diploma. This case study offers a glimpse of a pilot project designed to inform planning for Gateway 3 implementation (2010).

Throughout the Summer term of 2008, sixty Year 10 pupils from Ricards Lodge, engaged in research and preparation for their project, visiting a local stables to draw and photograph the horses and study their movements and anatomy. Two artists from Wimbledon College of Art sculpture department undertook their own research, meeting the National Theatre's props manager Allan Edwards to obtain advice on how best to construct the puppet and its moving parts. This preparation and research culminated in a two days work-shop in the college sculpture department, where students worked in teams to construct their designated parts of the horse. Some worked on legs, others constructed the intricate head and some focused on the saddle, reigns and stirrups! Throughout this process the students had in mind their final show at Wimbledon Theatre and were encouraged to plan, practice and refine their performance.

The project presented the young people with the opportunity to access Higher Education partners Wimbledon College of Art, where a visit to the dedicated space The Engine Room helped them experience learning in a different context. One student remarked that the experience had caused him 'to be patient, to work hard, to be willing to take direction and listen', another that 'it has been good to work in a different atmosphere and be taught by professionals'. The project accommodated a large number of students who could not always be fully engaged with all the tasks. The level of concentration and technical expertise required by the professional artists to meet the tight performance deadline meant that they had to be immersed in the process of construction rather than meet all the learning needs of such a diverse range of students. Pupils also required more rehearsal time at the theatre for their final performance. The final realisation was therefore a true partnership outcome for all concerned. See www.engineroomcogs.org and www.ricards lodge.merton.sch.uk for more details.

Performative professionalism in a 'Change' culture

In his useful account of the changing context of teacher education between 1976 and 2001, John Furlong distinguishes between the 'new professionalism' of the 1988 Green Paper set out by the newly incumbent Labour government and the 'competent practitioner' of the earlier period. Describing the various ironies inherent in the application of a competency tool (the Teacher Training Agency's (TTA) Standards framework[2]) for measurement of the dimensions of 'extended professionalism' (Hoyle, 1974), Furlong advocates a model of initial teacher training which seeks to develop 'these broader attributes that the government claims to be central to their vision for teachers of the future'

(Furlong, 2001:133). In light of the recent publication of a Standards mapping framework, this is ironic. Proposing alignment of the Professional Standards for the teacher workforce (necessary for the award of Qualified Teacher Status) with the Lifelong Learning Sector equivalent (QLTS), the document also describes a new set of Professional Attributes for the Diploma Practitioner. The areas in which Diploma teachers can enhance their knowledge, skills and understanding through professional development are identified as:

- applied learning
- assessment *for* and *of* learning
- collaborative working
- developing reflective practice
- generic learning skills
- information, advice and guidance and
- personalised learning[3]

Clearly, the Diploma Practitioner will need to perform on a different stage or set of stages to the ones they might be used to, and with a certain degree of reflexivity in the contractual terms and conditions established by consortia-employers. With the tension between current pay scales across different sectors, the fracturing of identities makes the 'possibility of commitment to broader professional goals more elusive' (Hargreaves and Goodson, 1996:11). Lorna Unwin's reflection on the specific problems faced by practitioners based in the lifelong learning sector is insightful:

> Vocational educators often have to work within different productive systems: those of their home institutions and of the workplaces they visit to monitor, support and assess learners. Their pedagogical expertise has to adapt to classrooms, workshops, simulated environments and workplace settings ... yet we are discussing a neglected, underpaid and undervalued community of professionals working in further education colleges and with private training providers. Not only are they paid less than school teachers, but their students are funded at a lower rate. (Unwin, 2008:18)

Whilst the development of Advanced Skills and Excellent Teacher status has offered school teachers career progression and financial reward, both roles are linked to performance-related pay systems. Reflecting on 'the reinvention of teacher professionalism', McCulloch comments that teachers 'expect accountability to take responsibility for improving their skills and subject knowledge, to seek to base their decisions on evidence of what works in schools.' The resulting frameworks peddled 'greater incentives for excellent performance' (McCulloch, 2001:115). In the context of the implementation of the diploma agenda, one is tempted to speculate that consortia-designed contracts might include financial incentives linked to the commercial outcomes of a project delivered in response to a live client brief. Perhaps more disturbing is the implication that learners who are facilitated to work alongside or shadow employers will also be working to a commercial imperative. This paradoxical movement between enhanced collaboration and collegiality (Hoyle, 1974), and competence-related individual performance may define the diploma practitioner as a composite – almost *mosaic* – rather than 'blended' professional born out of 'manufactured uncertainty' (Hargreaves and Goodson after Giddens (1995) 1996:11).

Diploma Practitioners: activist professionals for the knowledge economy?

The genesis of the 14-19 reforms should be viewed through the lens of the political and social change that is occurring at local and global level. Considerable critical attention has been paid to the impact of globalisation on education (Wood and Landry, 2008; Florida, 2008), with greater connectivity and mobility being one key feature of a highly stratified education system in which premium brand education is generally found in the most successful urban centres and 'parents want more flexibility, more control, and a more direct hand in shaping their child's education' (Florida, 2008:256). In this 'concrete context', there is a direct conflation between training models (and workplace strategies) adopted by employers, and models of professional development offered to educational professionals. Florida makes this link explicit:

> A recent study by the Gallup Organisation found that one way to improve schools is to better engage the teachers. A key to making schools more effective, the Gallup study shows is to involve the teachers integrally in all facets of the educational process, similar to the way successful and productive companies engage their employees. (Florida, 2008:255)

Interestingly, in their attempt to build local capacity, LSIS have mapped generic training frameworks, designed to introduce diploma practitioners to the pedagogic principles of consortia working, to so-called 'Inside the Workplace' events intended to 'gain an insight into their sector and the skills a potential young employee needs' (LSIS, 2009a:7). The model of vocational education which is implied here intrinsically problematises the concept of communities of practice. For if the diploma practitioner moves fluidly around a series of sub-sectors, forging relationships with employers, the idiosyncratic nature of their work places them in more dispersed networks, defined by Barton and Hamilton (2005) as 'more loosly-framed fields of social action ... weak on issues of power and conflict where groups do not share common goals and interests'. In this dis-articulated Bourdieuian field, the 'incomplete repertoire of shared resources' could also be 'the creative lifeblood of social change and challenge':

> Viewed like this, the social world is a long way from the prototypical community of practice. The social world is characterised by multiple membership, it has unresolved boundaries, with many different fluid communities of practice which exist in a variety of relationships to one another, both supporting and competing. (Barton and Hamilton, 2005:8)

If the field of operation is to have sufficient energy, attention must be paid to the development of strategies which will help to ensure commitment to personal and professional growth. One such strategic tool is a National Framework for Coaching and Mentoring, designed to 'help support 14-19 colleagues as they embed excellence in applied learning in day to day practice' (LSIS/CUREE, 2009b). The emphasis here is on the learner. As an example of a potentially altruistic appeal to professional ethics, there is a danger that the coaching framework might, as they say, serve as a 'means of social control rather than advancement'. Sally Power's 'imaginative professional' is a useful concept, and she cautions against indulgence in romanticised notions of the 'liberated' professional. Using C Stuart Mill's term 'sociological imagination' to examine 'the inner life and external career' of teachers, Power prompts us to ask a series of 'relational, temporal and dispositional' questions in order to foster the professional imagination:

> If professionals are to hold onto their sense of professionalism, they need creative and articulate responses to these changes rather than feelings of hopelessness and/or defensive reaction. The more sophisticated their understandings, the greater the chance of developing such creative and articulate responses. (Power, 2008:157).

Further research is needed on the relational, temporal and dispositional attributes of the diploma practitioner; the varieties of professional which will emerge from specific local and regional implementation contexts. As the interface between initial training, professional development and consortia practice begins to yield a range of narratives, the potential for invention and re-mapping will become evident. In this complex, rapidly shifting landscape, Judyth Sachs' (2003) *activist professional* may be a more energising conceptual persona. Influenced by Giddens' (1994) concept of 'active trust', 'activist professionalism means reinventing their professional identity and how they define themselves as teachers within their own schools and the wider education community'. Sachs continues:

> Activist teacher professionalism anticipates that teachers and others who are interested in education will be able to defend and understand themselves better ... [It is] not for the faint hearted. It requires risk taking and working collectively and tactically with others. Like any form of action, it demands conviction and strategy. However the benefits outweigh the demands. The activist teacher professional creates new spaces for action and debate, and in doing so improves the learning opportunities for all of those who are recipients or providers of education. (Sachs, 2003:153)

Notes

1 The process of documenting the first year of delivery also offers a strong model of practice; see the following web link for a short film as well as other detailed commentary from lead practitioners. www.emergingpractice.diploma-support.org/ConsortiaPlayer

2 The TTA was established in 1994 producing an initial set of standards in 1997 which were subsequently revised in 2002 and again in 2008. In 2008 the TTA received an extended remit and was formally re-designated as the Teacher Development Agency (TDA) with responsibility for workforce reform and development as well as initial training.

3 Diploma teachers must be able to relate positively to young people and their aspirations; be willing to help young people shape their own learning and their own futures... Best practice development is needed in particular for broadening teachers' repertoire of pedagogic skills to bring about more personalised, active learning that includes dialogue with learners about learning goals and processes.' *Excellence in Supporting Applied Learning.* Lifelong Learning UK and Training and Development Agency (TDA, 2007:5)

References

Barnett, R (2008) Critical professionalism in an age of super-complexity. In Cunningham, B (ed) *Exploring Professionalism.* Bedford Way Papers, Institute of Education

Barton, D and Hamilton, M (2005) Literacy, reification and the dynamics of social interaction. In Barton, D and Tusting, K (eds) *Beyond Communities of Practice: Language, Power and Social Context.* Cambridge University Press

Becher, T (1989) *Academic Tribes and Territories: intellectual enquiry and the culture of disciplines.* Open University Press, SRHE

Bourdieu, P (1984) *Distinction – a social critique of the judgement of taste.* Harvard University Press, USA

Florida, R (2005) *Who's Your City? how the creative economy is making where to live the most important decision of your life.* Basic Books, USA

Freidson, E (1994) *Professionalism Reborn – theory, prophecy and policy,* Polity Press

Fuller, A and Unwin, L (2002) Developing pedagogies for the contemporary workplace. In Evans, K and Hodkinson, P (eds) *Working to Learn*, Kogan Page

Furlong, J (2001) Reforming teacher education, re-forming teachers: accountability, professionalism and competence. In Philips, R and Furlong, J. *Education, Reform and the State: twenty-five years of politics, policy and practice.* Routledge

Halpin, D (2003) *Hope and Education: the role of the Utopian imagination.* Routledge/Falmer

Halpin, D. (2005) Educational Professionalism in an Age of Uncertainty: the emergence of eclectic and pragmatic teacher Identities, Paper presented at the International Symposium, Education Reform and Teachers, held at Hitotsubashi University, Tokyo, 12-13 November 2005

Hargreaves, A and Goodson, I (1996) Teachers' Professional Lives: aspirations and actualities. In I. Goodson and A. Hargreaves (eds) *Teachers' Professional Lives*, Falmer Press

Hargreaves, A with Goodson, I (2003) Educational Change and the crisis of professionalism. In Goodson, I and Hargreaves, *A Professional Knowledge, Professional Lives.* Open University Press

Hargreaves, A (2003) *Teaching in the Knowledge Society*, Open University Press

HM Government White Paper (2005) *14-19 Education and Skills.* The Stationery Office

Hoyle, E (1974) Professionality, Professionalism and Control in teaching. *London Educational Review*, Vol 3 (2)

Lave, J and Wenger, E (1991) *Situated Learning: legitimate peripheral action.* Cambridge University Press

Learning and Skills Improvement Service (2008) *Practitioner Guide to the Diploma*

Learning and Skills Improvement Service (2009) *Preparing you for Diploma delivery*

Learning and Skills Improvement Service (2009) *Connecting Up: building sustainability for 14-19 learning through coaching skills and techniques*

McCulloch, G (2001) The reinvention of teacher professionalism. In Philips, R and Furlong, J (eds) *Education, Reform and the State: twenty five years of politics, policy and practice.* Routledge

Nasta, T (2007) Translating National Standards into practice for the intial training of Further Education (FE) teachers in England. In *Research in Post- Compulsory Education*, Vol 12 (1), March 2007

Pine, J and Gilmore, J (1999) *The Experience Economy,* Harvard Business School Press, USA

Power, S (2008) The Imaginative Professional. In Cunningham, B (ed) *Exploring Professionalism*, Bedford Way Papers

Sachs, J (2003) *The Activist Teaching Profession*, Open University Press

Teacher Development Agency with Lifelong Learning UK (2007) *A Guide to Support the Professional development of Diploma Teachers*

Tomlinson, M (chair) (2004) *14-19 Curriculum and Qualifications Reform: final report of the working group on 14-19 reform.* DCSF

Unwin, L (2009) *Sensuality, sustainability and social justice: vocational education in changing times.* Based on an Inaugural Professional Lecture delivered at the Institute of Education, 4th Feb 2009

Whitty, G (2002) *Making Sense of Education Policy: studies in the sociology and politics of education.* Paul Chapman

The process of documenting the first year of delivery also offers a strong model of practice; see the following web link for a short film as well as other detailed commentary from lead practitioners. www.emergingpractice.diploma-support.org/ConsortiaPlayer

Appendix 1: Summary of Recommendations set out in 2005 White Paper: Education and Skills

16-19

- GCE A level structure to be simplified (from six to four units)

- Publication of results to be delayed to allow HE admissions processes to be clarified

- Extension Award to provide opportunities for higher level achievement

- A* grade for AS level

- Electronic transcripts setting out details of students' achievements in each unit to be made available

- Enhanced teacher assessment

A Strong foundation at Key Stage 3

- Strengthen performance in core subjects through Secondary National Strategy

- Introduce models of 'moderated teacher assessment' in 'key subjects'

- Record achievement at age 14 in a pupil profile

- Seek to ensure that 'more young people achieve Level 5 at Key Stage 3 in core subjects

Strong core 14 – 19

- More pupils to achieve 'functional competence' in English and Maths

- Toughen the GCSE achievement and attainment tables

- Create Routes to Success for All – introduce greater choice of what and where to study

- Retain GCSEs and A levels as cornerstones of the new system

- New specialised diplomas with exit points at three levels

- Give employers a greater say in the design of the new specialised diplomas through Sector Skills Councils

- Ensure that young people take qualifications when they are ready and not at a fixed age

Appendix 2: The Networked Teacher

Reproduced with kind permission of Alec Couros, University of Regina, December 2009, see www.educationaltechnology.ca for more details.

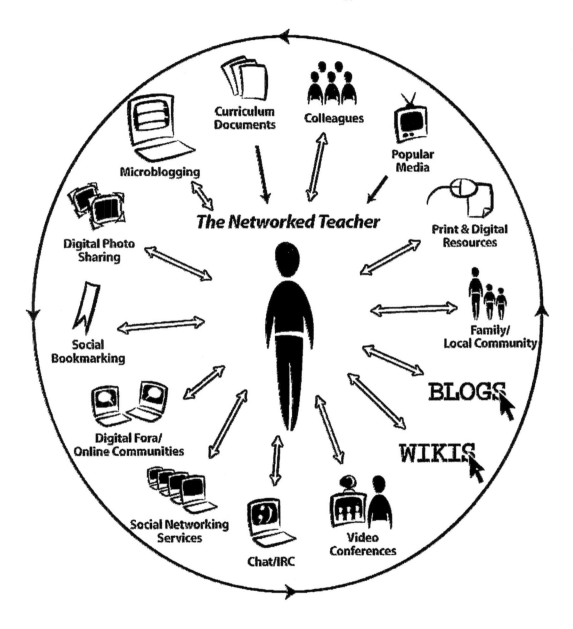

working together

London Bubble and educational psychologists working with Key Stage 1 pupils needing support

Speech Bubbles

Adam Annand

Hi Adam,

Hope you had a restful Christmas, I wanted to e-mail you and tell you something really amazing that happened thanks to the London Bubble sessions. One of the children in our group, a child who is painfully shy and has never taken part in an assembly, took part in the school Christmas play, to the amazement of his class teacher and his mother, who was very emotional. I thank you for giving me the chance to take part in the Bubble sessions. I have grown in confidence and feel I could run a session on my own.

Angie

In the office at London Bubble we have a little box of 'things to remind us why we do it' for reading whenever we are feeling tired, frustrated or if we are running out of steam, emotional states that are all too common for anybody working in the entertaining world of arts and education. This e-mail is the latest addition to that box. Angie is a learning mentor in a Southwark Primary school that is in the first term of a year long programme, Speech Bubbles. This chapter gives a flavour of that programme, an idea of what the individual sessions look and sound like, and describes how the programme is being developed through the shared input of drama practitioners, learning mentors and the educational psychology service. Some of the key markers in the journey to creating this unique programme of work are discussed, along with the knowledge and experience that has been drawn upon from previous partnership working.

Initially London Bubble was invited to create and deliver INSET for the learning mentors who work in the Southwark's Pupil Development Centres. The PDCs are described by Southwark NHS Primary Care Trust and Southwark Council as places with '...a common philosophy which is committed to enhancing the wellbeing of children, particularly in relation to their emotional and personal development.' Each centre is designed to meet the unique needs of the school. Many of the children are referred for social, emotional and behavioural reasons. Children may be brought out of their classroom for one or two sessions a week in the PDC. The centres are also places where those 'always' children, the ones who keep on working, keep on trying, can benefit from special recognition of their ongoing effort.

The learning mentors who run the centres are backed up by a team of advisers who co-ordinate training and provide direct support across the programme. The one and a half day INSET programme introduced drama techniques that non-specialists could use with small groups of primary children and included:

creative rule setting, drama games, hot-seating and story-acting. The learning mentors and advisers who attended the sessions reported back on how they had begun to use the techniques with groups of children and said they wanted more training.

Max Dixon, the Southwark educational psychologist with responsibility for the PDCs, was invited to visit London Bubble's other schools programmes with a view to our working together to develop a scheme of drama activity that would match the PDC's ethos and structure. She came to visit a Speak Out session in a Lewisham primary school where a small group of children had been referred to improve their communication skills. The children were telling their own stories and having them enacted by the rest of the group. What she also saw in that session was a model of partnership working, with drama practitioners, speech and language therapists and school staff working side by side.[1]

Following the session, Max and I discussed the need for a programme of work in Southwark that creatively addressed the borough's concerns about some Key Stage1 children's poor communication skills and the impact this had on speaking, listening and attention. It was important that this new programme would be attached to the already successful and established PDC initiative and take advantage of the enthusiasm of the learning mentors and advisers who had undergone the initial drama training.

The structure and approach of Speech Bubbles was devised with direct reference to the learning gained through the three years of the Speak Out programme. The Speak Out evaluation and assessments had pointed to the programme being most successful for children in Key Stage1 working in groups of less than ten, in 45 minutes sessions. We avoided disruption to the sessions by working four weeks either side of each half term, no sessions were lost because of school plays, school trips, end of term assemblies etc.

The drama workshop practice for Speech Bubbles was designed to respond to the evidence from Speak Out and other London Bubble programmes of in school work, especially our Creative Literacy programme which had been running in Southwark primary schools for three years[2]. At the core of this practice is an approach to creating, exploring and re-enacting stories that is deeply influenced by the work of Vivian Gussin Paley[3]. The other element that fed into this rich mix was the unique context of the PDC initiative, with its own distinct ethos and practice.

To help establish the conditions for positive partnership we began with a research and development day in the London Bubble rehearsal room. The day offered opportunities for each of the partners to play warm up games, create stories and take ownership of the programme. We came to shared understandings about the aims and approaches of the project and the responsibilities of the different partners. We discussed and shared our hopes and fears for the project and identified a shared vision of what success would look like. The learning mentors then invited the drama practitioners into the schools to get a sense of the environment of the PDC and find out more about the children they would be working with.

The importance of this relationship has been under some scrutiny within the world of arts and education since Ken Robinson identified the essential role being played by arts and education collaborations in the National Advisory Committee on Creative and Cultural Education (NACCCE) 1999 report *All our futures: Creativity, Culture and Education*. The report identified the challenge of training both artists and teachers to maximise the potential of these collaborations. In the eleven years since the report was published there has been an increase in the number of other adults working in schools and the role of learning mentors, teaching assistants and learning support assistants has been developing and growing. This programme recognises the role of these people and works with them to utilise their direct experience of the individual children and to continue developing their skills as effective practitioners.

The children are referred to Speech Bubbles because they need support with developing positive communication skills. For some children this might mean that they do not speak in class or that the teachers are not sure that they are understanding instructions. For others it could be that they struggle to maintain attention when their peers are talking. So we have a broad spectrum of children in these sessions, and perhaps you will recognise them if I give you a few composite examples:

- the child who comes into the room, sits down quietly and smiles if you catch his eye but then almost disappears from view for the duration of the session. He will answer a question if it is directed straight at him but you might find yourself not quite catching what he said. Perhaps, on a good day, you will have the time and space to get him to say it again. This child may have English as an additional language
- the child who seems to be getting on okay in the group, but physically freezes when she is asked even the most straightforward direct question. She doesn't ever choose to take a turn to speak but may be able

to engage in conversation with her peers. You might find yourself not involving this child in order to spare her what appears to be a deep level of discomfort

- the child who does not stop speaking, often quietly and often to herself, occasionally causing great disruption to the group with a loud comment about someone else. You might find yourself stepping up the levels of sanctions – with no discernible effect.
- the child who is interested in everything, distracted by anything new and cannot sit still. He might offer to take turns in joining in group talk or answer questions but often his input will be at best tangential or more likely about something else entirely

These referred children join a Speech Bubbles group for an academic year and take part in eight 45 minutes sessions per term. The sessions are planned and delivered by a team of practitioners: a drama specialist, a learning mentor and a PDC adviser. The team meet before and after every session to plan and evaluate together, with each member of the partnership bringing specialist knowledge of the school setting, of the children, of child development or of creative activity. In all we are working with 160 children in sixteen groups in eight schools per year.

The aims of the programme are explicit:

For the young people
Through a targeted programme of small group drama we aim to:

- increase their enjoyment in learning
- develop their communication skills
- improve their attention
- improve peer relationships

For the PDC co-ordinators and Learning mentors
Through the training, shared planning / delivery and evaluation programme we aim to support and develop their knowledge, experience and skill to plan and deliver appropriate drama activity

For the parents/carers
Through three active sessions through the year we aim to:

- increase their understanding of their children's learning
- support their positive relationships with the school setting
- engage them in positive and enjoyable communication

The sessions themselves are developmental over the course of the year and are tailored to address the needs of each group and the individual children. The sessions are also planned to maximise the skills, knowledge and experience of the team of practitioners working on each PDC. To give you a taste of what actually happens I will describe a fictional session that is a conglomeration of my experience of leading and watching sessions in all the schools we are working in. I hope this account will create a clearer picture in your mind than an account of a single session.

In a school in Southwark on a wet and cold Wednesday lunchtime, a drama practitioner, a learning mentor and a PDC adviser sit drinking tea in the staff room. They have in front of them a lesson plan, a dog-eared list of the children covered in pencil marks, a cuddly toy cat and some colourful laminated cards,

'Okay, they've definitely got the chant sorted out and they've got an action for every verse. Even James joined in last week, so this week we can start the session with me leading that.'

The learning mentor puts her name next to the first activity on the session plan and says, 'and then it's a game of Stop, Go, Jump, and Clap. I'd rather you led that,' she nods at the drama practitioner, 'and don't forget that they really like it when they can see that you are enjoying it too.' And so on, down to the end of the session plan, with names being marked next to activity and the occasional question for clarification.

'So we should write down all the different endings they come up with? They don't need to agree on just one?'

'Yes, seems right for them at this stage, but let's make a note that we are working towards them agreeing endings.'

The teacups are drained and the team are ready for action. As they make their way down the corridor to the Rainbow Room, they pass one little boy who asks them:

'Is it drama today?' and when they nod and smile, he beams, 'yes,' and punches the air with his fist before dashing off to tell his friend, 'it's drama!'.

The drama practitioner and the PDC adviser set up the Rainbow Room, moving the chairs and tables back to create a clear space on the floor. They sit down facing each other, with the cat and the laminated cards in a bag in front of the PDC adviser. The learning mentor comes into the room followed by a line of ten children. One girl, quite tall for her age, is sticking very close to the learning mentor and when they are asked to sit down in a circle, almost sits right on her lap.

'Let's start with our chant, everybody follow me and don't forget your actions. In Speech Bubbles we do listening.'

Everybody in the room copies the action of grasping an ear lobe and tilting the head to one side. Some of the children's actions are bigger, more expressive than others.

'In Speech Bubbles we take turns.'

Everybody mimes passing a package from one side to the next.

'In Speech Bubbles we act things out,' and everybody in the room takes up their own exclamatory gesture, looking like a room full of Shakespearian actors in the middle of a tragic soliloquy.

As the next activity begins, the girl stays stuck fast to the learning mentor, and when it is her turn to say her name and something she remembers about Speech Bubbles, she answers very quietly,

'My name is Nazmin, and I remember a cat,' and the toy cat is pulled out of the bag. The boy next to her spins around on his bottom and speaks.

'My name is Malachi, and I remember we do listening,' and as he says it all the group tilt their heads to one side and grasp an ear lobe.

And so it goes round the circle with only one hiccup; when it comes to Isaac who says,

'I wanted to remember the same thing Malachi remembered.'

'Well that's alright you can remember it too.'

'Yes but I wanted to remember it first.'

'We would like to hear it again,' and although he doesn't look completely convinced, he says,

'My name is Isaac and I remember good listening.' Once again the whole group grasp an ear lobe and tilt their heads to one side.

'Okay, who can remember what we do next, hands up please?' says the PDC adviser, scanning the whole group and pointing to a boy whose hand is raised, but only just,

'We play a game.'

'Thank you Luke, great turn taking. Today we are going to play Stop, Go because you were all so good at it last week. Okay, on your feet and start walking around the room, fill up all the spaces.'

All but one of the children gets up and starts walking around the room. The group are concentrating on filling up all the spaces and listening intently for the next instruction. Nazmin moves around the room, sticking closely to the learning mentor. Isaac cannot quite manage to keep walking and with every third step or so he breaks into a little jog. When he hears the drama practitioner call out 'Stop' he freezes, with his arms high in the air and his legs spread wide apart. The challenge for him will come in the next part of the activity, when 'stop' means go and 'go' means stop. Last week he struggled to follow the instructions, although he enjoyed the game.

The game progresses and the children work hard to follow the reversed instructions. Two or three minutes in, the learning mentor stops when she should go, the concentration is broken and the room bubbles with laughter. The one child who didn't join in at the beginning of the game is now up on her feet, not quite joining in but moving around the room when it's time to Go.

'Okay, now find a partner. Last week we got to the point in the story where the boy looked in the mirror. Choose one of you to be 'A' the other to be 'B'. All As put your hands up, great, well done! Everybody, sit down where you are whilst Dave and Anne show you what we are going to do next.'

The children watch intently as the learning mentor and PDC adviser demonstrate a pairs mirroring activity. The two adults hold the attention of the group, working hard to mirror exactly the other person's movement. Now it is the children's turn, and they stand facing each other.

'Don't forget to make eye contact with your partner and start slowly so that they can follow you.'

Around the room, physical conversations are beginning to take place, some pairs begin gently and build up to more complicated shapes and gestures, while with others the movement is almost imperceptible. One pair of boys develops the mirroring into a sequence of complicated martial arts moves. They look a little apprehensive, unsure whether this is allowed, until they get the adult approval they want: 'Make sure you don't go faster than your partner can follow ... excellent following ... well done.'

When everybody has had a go, the pairs are given an opportunity to show their moves to the whole group, and the eager audience of peers are tasked to watch carefully to see if they can tell who is leading. Precious, who has had very little to say in the session so far, guesses correctly every time and is clearly very pleased with her skills of observation. Now, for the first time in a session, she is brave enough to offer an opinion,

'I liked Malachi's karate moves.' A nod of approval ripples around the group.

Now that the group are warmed up and ready to work creatively together, the session moves on with a recap of the Cat story they worked on last week. Using the laminated narrative cards[4] as visual prompts, the group recall who is in the story, where it is set, when it is happening and what has happened. When it comes to the blue 'The End' card, the group don't know the answer.

'I wonder how you would like it to end?' the PDC adviser asks.

Five children's hands shoot up,

'Hold onto those thoughts – don't tell me just yet, I want everybody to have a chance to think about it.'

The children are split up into three groups, each with an adult equipped with pen and paper. The groups huddle, heads together, and start to discuss possible endings. The adult writes down their favourite possibility. This seems to be going very well until in one of the groups a behaviour pattern is repeated:

'But I wanted to say the same as Malachi!' says Isaac, as he sits there with his eyes downcast and arms crossed. This time it is Malachi who sorts it out:

'That's Okay, we can share the idea.' Isaac looks straight at him,

'Thanks, but can the Cat run away at the very end?'

'Yes alright, that makes it even better,' and Malachi and Isaac knock their knuckles together and smile.

The group come back together, and this time they sit around a small square that has been marked out on the floor in masking tape,

'Well done everyone, before we act out all the different endings who can remind us of the rules of the story square?'

'You sit outside until it's your turn to go in.'

'You can make the sounds of things, like the traffic – beep'

'You have to do the things that are read out.'

'Great, and what about when I say 'whoosh', what do you do then?' All together the group do a collective whoosh, moving their arms across the front of their bodies,

'Everybody who is acting has to sit down and new people come in.'

The drama practitioner chooses the first ending,

'Okay, this one was Precious and Mohamed's idea.' And as he looks across at Precious and Mohamed they sit up a little taller, with a small smile playing on their lips.

Isaac calls out, 'I want mine to be first!'

The learning mentor moves to sit next to him.

'In Speech Bubbles we take turns,' he says and repeats the passing movement from earlier. Isaac looks up at him a little unsure, 'and yours and Malachi's fantastic ending will be acted out.'

Isaac accepts the point, and the drama practitioner carries on:

'The cat settled down and fell asleep in front of the fire.'

One child jumps up and settles in the centre of the square as if a sleeping cat, and with a look from the drama practitioner, two more children come into the square and wave their arms up and down, being a fire. Around the square all the others make the crackling sound of a log fire.

'The end. Whoosh.'

The story endings are all acted out. Some are longer than others and one has the cat running away again, leaving the possibility for further episodes. As each story ending is offered to the group for re-enactment, the authors grow in stature, sit up straighter and make more eye contact. The session is brought to an end with the whole group creating an imaginary shower that washes off all the characters from the story. The children are led out of the room by the learning mentor.

The drama practitioner and PDC adviser set the room up ready for the second group of the afternoon, ten more children from Year 1 and Year 2. This group includes James, who has not yet spoken in any session. The nearest he got was last week, when he mouthed the words of the chant. He has been referred because he chooses not to talk in class. His mum is concerned and also a little confused because, as she tells the school, 'he talks all the time at home.'

The session starts in the same way as the first, and James, as expected, silently mouths the words to the chant. The children sit down in a circle and take it in turns to say their name and something they remember about the sessions. All is going well, everybody takes their turn and then it comes around to James,

'My name is James, and I remember that last week we had to do Stop and Go, and the cat nearly got run over...' – he is not ready to stop talking yet – 'and I acted out the part of the tree in the wind.'

The three adults in the room are visibly shocked for a moment, amazed by this breakthrough, but they contain their excitement and thank James for his input.

'Well remembered James.'

Later on when the session is over and all the children have left to go back to class, the team burst into laughter and give themselves a collective high five.

'I nearly jumped up and gave him a big hug when he spoke.'

'Me too, but can you imagine the pressure that would put on him?'

'It worked too; if we had given it too much attention then he might have been overwhelmed for the rest of the session. He just carried on joining in; it was like a dam had broken. I'll tell his teacher at the end of the day.'

The session evaluation goes on for the next twenty minutes, checking how each individual child did and what activities were most engaging, and planning for the following week's session. The debate in the evaluation concentrates on Nazmin's continued need for physical proximity to an adult and Grace in group two, who this week was struggling to follow simple instructions and found it hard to concentrate in the mirroring exercise. A draft session plan is devised for next week's session which attempts to respond to these issues and the needs of the whole group. The team disband, the learning mentor off to tidy up the Rainbow Room and set up for tomorrow's activities, the drama practitioner going to run an evening youth theatre and the PDC adviser to plan for other sessions in other schools.

The session described is fairly typical. It has a clear structure and routine that the children recognise and can feel confident within. It uses games and exercises that are fun to take part in and which promote positive attention, listening and turn taking. It has scaffolding activities that develop the children's ability to communicate positively, both verbally and non-verbally. Through the use of story telling and story acting, it gives the children a sense of ownership and pride in the content of the sessions. Across the term and year, the sessions will include a range of games, action songs and different drama techniques. Some weeks the children will be acting out their own individual stories, in others the stories will be group devised. The sessions may also include traditional tales or stories drawn from the great canon of children's literature at our disposal. Practitioners use hot seating, teacher-in-role, soundscapes, image theatre and aspects of forum theatre to explore the stories. They use toys and puppets to create characters the children can respond to, talk for and interact with.

In the first term's evaluation, all the partners came together for half a day to share the learning from each of the eight schools. They reported back on successes in terms of the children's communication and the different practitioners' skills, knowledge and confidence. The testimony on children's development reported by the different practitioners reviewed what had changed in their engagement in the sessions and also changes in their wider school engagement. Remember – this evidence is being collected after only eight sessions with each group. They noted:

- children were able to keep their attention throughout the session. Children waiting their turn and listening to their peers. Children who at the beginning would always look away now making eye contact with adults and peers. Improvements in their confidence to offer ideas and take part in positive activity, both within the sessions and back in the classroom
- four children who choose not to talk or who use minimal language in school have spoken in Speech Bubbles sessions

The different groups of practitioners are also reporting back on the success of the programme in developing their own confidence and skill in working creatively with small groups, with Angie's quote at the start of the chapter being a prime example

- for the PDC advisers: the programme is giving them access to a new set of creative drama approaches. The collective planning and evaluation comes as a relief in a working week when they have to plan many sessions by themselves
- for the drama practitioners: the opportunity to work in close partnership and build up a long term relationship with a group of children is welcomed. Much of their work in schools is short term or one off sessions with no real possibility of seeing individual children's progress. The shared evaluation of sessions gives them the opportunity to learn from the learning mentors and PDC advisers about child development
- for the learning mentors: within the supportive team they can develop their skills and confidence in planning and running creative activity with small groups. These skills are being used to enhance activities in other sessions

This partnership approach to working requires a degree of mutual understanding, respect, and willingness for the partners to generously share their knowledge and practice and be open to learning from each other's experience. Previous research into the relationship between artists and educationalists has also identified this positive relationship as having a direct impact on the children,

A creative partnership where teacher and artist share equal status provides a model of teamwork, respect and mutual support. This is mirrored in pupils' engagement with each other, and consequently in the level of their achievement.[5]

At the time of writing we are midway through the first year of this programme and plans are being put in place for developing and improving Speech Bubbles in the year ahead. We commissioned an action research project on the setting up of the programme and are using the findings of the ensuing report to refine the structure, training and practice. The report, *The art of building creative relationships*[6] sets the programme the challenge of extending the good practice of partnership building to the wider school community and increasing the involvement and connection of classroom teachers and parents.

This programme of work sits within the wider context of London Bubble's creative offer and our desire to make meaningful high quality theatre with and for our community. Each week in Speech Bubbles children in Key Stage 1 are creating beautiful and touching moments of theatre, told and re-enacted with an audience and cast of peers, learning mentors, PDC advisers and drama practitioners.

Notes

1 An evaluation report on the three year practice and research project 'Speak Out' can be downloaded from www.londonbubble.org.uk/dostuff/inschools

2 Creative Literacy was funded by the Sir John Cass Foundation and was delivered from 2006 – 2009.

3 In 2002 London Bubble hosted a conference 'The Drama of Children' at the British Library. The conference included a key note by Vivian Gussin Paley.

4 Narrative cards – *Speaking and Listening through Narrative* (2006) Black Sheep Press, Keighley UK

5 *The Art of the Animateur Animarts* 2003. Available from www.animarts.org.uk

6 The research was undertaken by Paula Robinson for Birkbeck College, University of London and funded by Knowledge Connect.

From child script idea to professional performance

Quicksilver Theatre: Primary Voices, playwriting in schools programme

Carey English

I felt like a director, like I could change characters' emotions

We felt respected for our ideas

I didn't like being interrupted by playtime

Quicksilver Theatre makes new plays and participatory projects for children and young people. Throughout its thirty odd years Quicksilver has sought to inspire children, to empower them to communicate, to relish their innate creativity and be responsible for their learning. Three core participatory age appropriate programmes focus on play, storytelling or playwriting; we give children the tools to express themselves in a powerful and memorable way, and the means to be heard.

Playwriting in schools can be a challenge because few primary school teachers have detailed specialist and technical knowledge about how to write a play. Plays should be written to be performed. Without the performance element or at least the possibility of it, writing plays can be a pretty dismal activity. If children perform their own writing, the focus on writing is defused, but the introduction of theatre practitioners into the process can cystallise that focus.

> We can't cover it like that, with all the will in the world it's never going to be as good as actors stood there acting out what you have written. It was just so powerful for the children to have the actors in the classroom and there was one point that I will never forget – we had the tables on one side of the room and the actors on the other side and they stormed out of the classroom and had to walk about a metre past the children and they were shaking with excitement they were so engrossed in the drama that was going on. The actor who was doing it had actually walked so close to them – it was really amazing. (Classroom teacher)

153

A number of theatre organisations work in this way, among them Soho Theatre, Scene and Heard and Hampstead Theatre. Primary Voices, Quicksilver's playwriting in schools programme, began in 2006 as a project to discover what really matters to 8-11 year olds and integrate that into Quicksilver's theatre productions. We have worked with schools in Hackney, Camden and Islington, north and east London. The process was so artistically invigorating and of such obvious benefit to the children that it has become core to Quicksilver's participatory work and a production in itself.

We encourage the children to be adventurous and imaginative in what they write, and are not prescriptive of content or form. The range of plays has been extraordinary – from explorations of friendship, puppy love, and daft fantasy, to hard hitting social dramas of bullying, betrayal and death. The importance of family and friendship groups predominates. All genres are here: adventure, sci-fi, spy stories, comedy, horror, romance, spoof, rom-com, thriller, social realism, even a celebration of the Ancient Greeks. Often the writing is bare and to the point and sometimes it belies the age of the writer. Take this example from one of the schools Quicksilver has worked with:

The Bad Boys by Jordan Gibson-Walden (aged 10)
© Benthal School London E8

SCENE 1
(Ace and Nicholas are sitting on the wall outside Ace's house)

Nicholas: (in slang) So anyways how is your girl?

Ace: (in slang) Yeah fams she bless, what about your mum?

Nicholas: Yeah man she's cool

(Nicholas walks to Steven)

Nicholas: Oi! Come here

(Steven didn't go to Nicholas)

Ace: Nicholas what are you doing?

Nicholas: Don't worry

(Nicholas went to Steven)

Nicholas: What you got for me?

Steven: Nothing

(Nicholas punches Steven in the face)

Nicholas: (Takes his chain and his phone) Nice phone mate thanks

Ace: (Takes his air forces trainers and his money) Great Trainer, oh yeah thanks for the money

Steven: Watch when I catch you your dead

Ace and Nicholas: (Running) Ha Ha Ha

SCENE 2

(Nicholas is at home with his Mum)

Mum: Are you ok love?

Nicholas: Yes mum I'm fine how about you?

Mum: I'm fine

Nicholas: Mum

Mum: Yes darling

Nicholas: Can Ace come round to our house?

Mum: Yes darling and ask him does he want any dinner

Nicholas: Ok Mum

Nicholas: (phones Ace) Ace do you want to come round my yard?

Ace: Yeah fams

Nicholas: Oh yeah do you want dinner?

Ace: Yeah man I'm starving

Ace: (Rings the door bell) It's me

Mum: (Doors open) Alright love? So how is your Mum and Dad?

Ace:(Nicely) Yeah she's okay, how are you?

Mum: I'm fine

Nicholas: Stop chatting up my mum and get to my room

Ace: Alright man just chill

SCENE 3

(Nicholas changing his life to be a good boy)

Nicholas: Ace I'm not being a bad boy or sooner or later we'll get stabbed or shot, I'm going back to school.

Ace: Fine, you be like that

Nicholas: Yeah I will be like that

Ace: Don't you like this life?

Nicholas: No because when we get shot we won't have a life.

Ace: Are we still friends?

Nicholas: Yeah

Ace: Alright then bless

Nicholas: Safe

SCENE 4

(Ace is with his friends)

Ace: Were is my money?

Nicholas: Oi Ace   leave the kid alone

Ace: You're back

Nicholas: I just came to see how you are

Ace: Oh Cool

Nicholas: What been going on while I was away?

Ace: Nothing

Nicholas: Have you seen Steven yet?

Ace: No have you?

Nicholas: No

Ace: So how is school?

Nicholas: Yeah it's cool

Ace: Is it ?

Nicholas: Yeah

Ace: I haven't seen you in time

Nicholas: I know, how's life on the road?

Ace: It's not the same without you

Nicholas: Ain't it?

Ace: No

SCENE 5

(Nicholas is with Ace because it's summer holidays)

Ace: Look there is Steven

Nicholas: Oh yeah

Steven (In slang) You mans want beef

Nicholas: No

Ace: Yeah what you going to do about it?

Steven: Kill you

(Jamie comes in)

Jamie: You're dead

Nicholas: Ok I believe you

Jamie: You should

Ace: Get out of our ends

Jamie: Is it now

Steven: Shall we deal with them?

Jamie: Come then

(Steven and Jamie stabbed Nicholas and Ace)

Jamie: Good

Steven: Serves them right

SCENE 6

(Nicholas and Ace's funeral is on the same day, lots of people gathering round the coffings)

Mum: Bye son you'll always be in my heart and you Ace.

The writer is clearly making a stand against knife crime. The play's language and grammar is idiosyncratic, the content strong and the voice of the writer is powerful and memorable.

So how does it all work?

For the initial format we are indebted to Jon Lloyd, then at Soho Theatre and currently artistic director of Polka Theatre. We have commissioned workshop scripts, added an extra workshop and brought our own style of delivery. Currently Primary Voices works like this – over a period September to January we run the following:

INSET

Playwriting Workshop 1: Character, dialogue, story and stage directions
Playwriting Workshop 2: Structure of a play and layout
Playwriting Workshop 3: Content and genre
Independent writing period
Script development workshops
Design workshop
Rehearsal visit to meet the creative team
Primary Voices Showcase

It is important to establish a strong relationship with teachers on the programme so the INSET session is an opportunity to hear about the teachers' experience and concerns as well as discussing how we can work together in the classroom. Teachers are encouraged to contribute and to praise the children during the workshop. They know their children best and can support us to get the most from them. Also we need to know about classroom protocols and codes of behaviour so that we are working as a team. There are also tiny details like having paper and pencils ready, as well as moving the furniture because the children will talk a lot and need to sit in groups. Each group will write as a team. We can also find out whether any child in the class has special needs. The first and second workshops each take up a whole morning.

The first workshop focuses on getting the children to write a scene and is led by a theatre director with two actors. For continuity these actors will also perform in the showcase. The workshop begins with a demonstration of a specially written scene. The scene is written by Pete Lawson, a playwright and TV scriptwriter with extensive experience of planning and running workshops for people of all ages. We asked him to write a scene that could establish three characters and include a lot of information about all the characters – their desires, fears, weaknesses, secrets – and sets up relationships and settings. The characters Jay and Dee are baby buddies but now they have reached Year 7 Dee is growing up faster than Jay and this causes conflict, particularly where Mark, the captain of the football team, is concerned. Dee really likes Mark and in trying to impress him has told him one of Jay's big secrets – the betrayal is monumental. Immediately the children are drawn in – this is stuff of the playground, a familiar dilemma. It helps that the characters are just that bit older than the children watching – they all aspire to be older.

The actors perform, script in hand. This is a key message: this piece of paper with words on it is the starting point for an actor's performance. The actors perform a second time with stage directions read aloud. When the children write new stage directions of their own and see them performed the penny begins to drop – they have power as writers. Theatre professionals are taking them seriously to the point of 'he faints and falls on the floor' or 'he cries like a girl and runs away' or even 'she shouts woohoo and does the Worm'. The latter works especially well when the actress is an acrobat and can actually do a perfect Worm (a street dance move).

Then it is on to character. In groups the children discuss each character. I have learnt that it is very effective to give children the chance to talk together about a question before giving an answer. This is a great way to encourage the group dynamic of each group of children who will later be a writing team. So, what do they know about each character from the scene they have watched? The children shift up another gear when responding to questioning and begin to build each character's description from the information they have. What are their hates, fears, most wanted thing in the world? What is their domestic life like, their family? There is lots of shared thinking going on as they move on from what they know about the character to extra features they imagine about the character. Everything they say is scribed on big pieces of paper as the picture of each character builds up. To get them writing through the voice of a character, the children write a very short character monologue which the actors perform.

> The structure that the guys used for character and plot development was really useful – the questions they used as prompts, we use those now if we do script work with the children... (Classroom teacher)

We talk about dialogue; can you hear any patterns in the way the characters talk? What different rhythms do the characters have? Any catchphrases?

With all the information which the children have gathered collectively displayed on large paper around the classroom, the children have comprehensive information to draw on. Then it is on to actually writing a scene. Two children in each group scribe the scripts – one for each actor – and all contribute ideas. A script is a working document, eg stage directions need to look different to speech so the actor knows what to say. Therefore they need to use italics, capitals or brackets. It is harder to learn that in a classroom without actors. Interestingly, what they remember most from their Year 5 study of playwriting is how to lay out the page. This reflects what some teachers have said about their own teaching of play writing.

> I would have looked at the words they were using and the layout rather than the content, I guess. What the actors did was really bring it home (writing) to entertain rather than another piece of writing.

The scene might follow the one they have just watched or they might choose to write a parallel scene or a scene earlier in the action. They talk a lot and need to be close to each other to hear each other easily so each group sits around one small table.

> ...the talk – was really important for improving writing process and also helping them to feel that there are occasions that they can write as they speak because often as teachers we are telling them not to write as they speak. It gave them some confidence, which was really nice.

It surprises me that children are encouraged to talk in Early Years and build communication skills only to often be told to work in silence as they move further up the school. When they talk in small groups they are collaborating creatively, accepting and building on one another's ideas. With experience, the workshop leader and actors learn to strike a sensitive balance between supporting groups with open questions and advice, and the need to hold back and let the children's creative force flow.

The first workshop concludes with the performance of all the scenes the children have written.

A week later the second workshop takes place. The purpose is to write several scenes, ie a small play. To begin the actors perform three monologues. Pete Lawson has written three characters in a school setting, – Luke and Chantelle who are cousins and a Welsh geography teacher who is preparing his class for a school trip involving camping and climbing Ben Nevis. Clearly well beyond the regular experience of inner city London children! These monologues and the scene in workshop one were researched with Year 7 and Year 8 children. They are accurate in universal preoccupations of prepubescent friendship, self image, football, fashion etc and in contemporary language and music. They are humorous which really helps to engage the children's interest. Again the children examine the characters in detail collectively and all their suggestions are scribed and displayed where everyone can see them.

After quickly revisiting character, stage directions and dialogue the writing happens in bite sized chunks, beginning with setting and character – who is in the scene? Where are they?

What matters to them right now? The children have plenty to work from. Luke cannot swim, Chantelle may be afraid of the dark, Chantelle is scared of heights though she really wants to prove herself and Mr. Jones seems more star struck by singer Tom Jones than by being an A1 outward bound expedition leader. There is plenty that could go wrong.

For the second scene something really good or bad happens to one or two of the characters. This develops and is resolved in the third scene. The children make a choice about how it all ends – a neat wrap up or leaving some mystery or choice for the audience to ponder.

Again all their writing is performed at the end of the session – a Herculean feat from the actors, who have seven to nine plays to perform, picking their way through eccentric handwriting and responding to requests for singing, acrobatics, dance, anything the children throw at them. All sorts of scenarios appear – bus breakdowns, motorway accidents, getting lost in the dark, falling off cliffs into torrential waters, breaking a leg on top of the mountain, or meeting Tom Jones there on the mountain. The cousins tease, argue, set each other up, rescue, console, admit secrets, forgive, blame, lie, laugh, weep inconsolably, make up etc.

The third workshop is still in development. Previously we have given children and teachers guidelines for content and genre but some practical work on producing scripts in a range of genres will help teachers and children get off to an even stronger start. By now the children are playwrights, this much they have just demonstrated. Then we tell them we would like to produce some of their plays professionally and we invite and encourage them to write more plays. We encourage them to really use their imaginations. They can write a true life drama or it can be fantastical. We stress that it is important to write what they like, not to worry about how to stage it. Staging it is the challenge they are giving us. The only limits are that the play can have up to five characters and it needs to be about five minutes long. We trust them to lay it out properly. We trust them to give us characters we can work with. The children can write in small groups – up to five in a group or on their own.

Three weeks later over one hundred scripts arrive. When selecting the ten plays for performance we look at character, dialogue, stage directions, structure, originality, quality of drama and potential for staging. There is a team of readers to ensure we have wide consensus of the plays chosen. We also have to be conscious of achieving a good representative spread of subject matter. Some scripts might have holes in them but it is clear that the writers have the answer in their heads. For example, *Four Wheels and a Plank of Wood* has very clear setting and characters, a good story developing and fluid dialogue –

Four Wheels and a Plank Of Wood by Oliver Hilferty (aged 10)
(c) Princess May School London E8

David – he likes skate boarding and is a member of the Hackney Skate Board Club.

Tom – best friends with David. He also likes skate boarding but he doesn't have a board.

Mrs Smith – Tom's mum

Boy – owner of the stole skate board

Scene one

Location – Hackney Skate Boarding Club – David is practising and Tom is watching.

Tom (shouting)   Hey David, I bet you can't do an Indy 180!

David goes up to the Quarter Pipe (QP) and does an Indy and a 180 degree spin. Easy.
I bet you can't

Tom   Of course I can't. I don't have a board.

David   Well, use mine.... (*David pushes his board forward*)
                    And you might want these as well (*David hands Tom a set of pads*)

Tom   Thanks

David   And try not to mess my board up

Tom (*strapping on the pads, replies sarcastically*) Oh, thanks for the support

David   Just hurry up and crack your skull!

Tom   Hey!

David   Only joking.

Tom   Here I go

(*Tom goes up the QP and does an Indy 180 but his board hits the ramp and he crashes.
He's groaning and clutching his hand*) Oww, Awww, my hand.

David (*runs up to Tom and urgently asks him*) Tom give me your hand ... does that hurt?

Tom (*still groaning*)No

David   How about that?

Tom (*shouting in pain*) OWWWW

David   OK, don't worry, it's only sprained.

Tom (groaning)   Aw man.

David   Hang on; I know where to get some bandages.

David (*putting bandages on Tom*) Here you go. Does that feel better?

Tom (*still groaning*) Kind of.

Scene two
Location – Outside Tom's house

David	Hey Tom, how's your hand?
Tom	Kind of OK
David	Hey look at that! It's a sign for a skate competition and the 1st prize is £1000
Tom	Are you going to enter?
David	Yeh, of course. How about you?
Tom	What do you mean, I don't have a board.
David	Oh yeah, sorry I forgot.

Working with a dramaturg can help the child get the next draft they want. *Four Wheels and A Piece of Wood* was unfinished but the writer had drawn a storyboard and had simply run out of time to put it all down on paper. Other plays may be overwritten and need paring down, the relationship between characters may need sharpening, dramatic tension needs to build. Asking the writer questions about characters and story can help this.

The child writers then come to the theatre to meet the creative team to talk about their plays. This engages them in a real professional relationship. Serious questions need answering. How do you see this character? Why does this happen? What is this character's home like? What is great here is that the child writers, the production team and the actors are working together on a level playing field, they are bona fide artistic collaborators. Their input can have great impact. For example, the stage directions for Big Babies read

Scene One
Wizard family house. 18 year old Michaela has finished high school and is practising her spells in the magic attic – spell books floating around, cups floating, noises everywhere. To the wizards this is normal, they don't worry. Her dad comes in.

Scene two
Mum. Michaela, Paris (10) and James (191/2) are talking in the living room. Everyone looks at Dad venting his anger.

Questions reveal that Mum is not a wizard, that Michaela is punky – small details that can have a big effect. Mum becomes otherworldly in a 'normal' wizard world and Michaela is emphasised as the rebellious teenager in conflict with her father.

The child writers also decide on a by-line for their play to go in the programme and to use as a brief for a poster. Each class involved is invited to create a poster for the play chosen from their class. We explain what information a poster needs to convey and how it needs to attract the eye from a distance. One poster for each play is selected for a Front of House display at the theatre. Quicksilver plans to develop this area with input from a graphic artist.

Visiting the theatre to see the plays is a highlight for all the children:

> The most rewarding part of the project was watching our play at the opening because it made me really happy and proud of our performance. (Child member of the audience)

The 'our' here refers to the play from their school. All the children feel proud of the play from their school.

> And the response when the plays were announced even before they went on, the response was to clap and cheer because it was 'here comes ours!' so it was 'ours' rather than 'here comes hers'... (Class teacher)

Seeing plays in a small theatre was novel for some.

> It was something they had never seen before. Like we went into the theatre and everyone was like 'What is this?' – 'It's a theatre'. Because they had only ever seen like big musical productions and they'd only ever understood that that was what a theatre was. They were really like 'Ooh, we've been to a theatre!' They loved it! (Class teacher)

All the children involved in the workshops plus the rest of their year group come to see the plays and the invitation is extended to other schools. Because the plays are written by peers the theatre experience is entirely relevant and accessible to the audience. In the next Primary Voices project, we will open up the experience to many more audiences from other schools.

Families of the writers also come to see the plays; parents often coming to the theatre for the first time see the child in a completely new light and are immensely proud. Each writer receives a further certificate celebrating the premiere performance of their play and a bound copy of their script. Putting children at the heart of the creative process is very rewarding. There are big dividends for the children's education and personal development.

> They were writing as fast as they could, as well as they could, some of them didn't want to go out to play, you know, really, they wrote really well, it was really nice to see ... they were really proud of the children in their class's work ... You

know, I've not seen any of them laugh like that, it was really nice ...' To see them making really good progress and that being recognised was really, really nice ... just how professional it all was, from the moment we signed up onto it, right through to the final performance, you know, how much effort was put into it by everybody at Quicksilver, and how seriously the children's scripts were taken and treated...

The Primary Voices process connects with children who often don't get involved.

...the children who wouldn't pay attention as much were actively involved in listening they were actually following and watching it ... it was a much more intimate experience to writing because these actors, professionals, are actually going to do what we write down. And so they got really excited about trying out loads of ideas and they can explore their imagination a bit more. So it was more intimate in that aspect ... they were just a lot more open and creative ... I think when they write things they are a little embarrassed about what they could potentially put in it – but because they were actors who will do anything or everything and they reminded the students of that – so that pushed them ... even the children who don't get that involved were really excited to be writing.

... seeing what a difference it makes in the children's attitudes towards writing and just being more open minded to being creative definitely makes me want to have more workshops and programmes ... it encourages them to want to be able to write. (Class teachers)

I was interested that the teacher had never seen the children laugh in the way they did here. We can never underestimate the importance of joy. It is a potent creative life affirming force.

Responding to the children's plays artistically is very challenging – ten disparate plays need to be brought together in a cohesive whole and every writer's vision must be honoured. It is very hard work, a marathon for all concerned – if actors can have fifteen to twenty roles, imagine what the stage managers must do!

We have done Primary Voices three times and are gearing up for a fourth. On the early projects we presented twenty plays in total – two plays from each school – using rehearsal blocks, sound and projection to set scenes and minimal costumes. More recently we scaled down to ten plays and built up production values working with a designer and composer/musician. The play list included the wizard home of *Big Babies*, a *Time Machine* in which characters watched themselves as babies and aged 32 in an airport, journeys on two different buses, various classroom, dinner hall and playground scenes, a shop, various bedrooms, a 1940s train station and a grand mansion, a haunted house, and a haunted chip shop with a chicken that berates customers for ordering chicken and chips.

Much can be done physically and all of it requires commitment and versatility from the actors. Designer Darren Goad created two tall white multi-faceted towers decorated with every kind of picture frame in black outline. Concealed amongst these were various pop up devices which revealed themselves as the show went on, to help create all these different settings. Light and sound certainly help to carve out the picture. Manoeuvering the towers creates different shapes and areas on the stage – they are also a logistical nightmare and took a long time to get right. The time machine was the most challenging to achieve. We used the celebrated Forkbeard Fantasy trick of 'breaking the celluloid divide' where actors physically interact with film, literally stepping in and out of it. Once the actors had stepped into the time machine they were on film. They watched themselves as babies – we used humanettes – baby puppets with full size human heads. Playing themselves as 32 year olds seemed a doddle after that.

The wizard home was full of magic spells, the haunted chip shop specified floating chips and talking chickens, all of which lends itself to ultra violet lighting effects which really worked well.

Having a musician on board really helped to pull the piece together. His underscore for each play really helped to create atmosphere and tension. He composed a rap which opened and closed the show, about the children's act of participating. He also acted as MC in between plays as well as providing the music.

Some of the actors were also involved in the workshops so the children recognise them at the Showcase. Actors are a really strong focus for the children. It is so important that the children feel respected by them from the start of the workshop process, that they feel we are there for them. It makes them feel special, it makes them open up, and it makes them creative

> I think when they write things they are a little embarrassed about what they could potentially put in it – but because the actors will do anything or everything and they reminded the students of that – so that pushed them. (Class teacher)

We follow through on this at the showcase; the actors meet and greet the children and bring the children into the auditorium and they are there waiting for the children when they leave the auditorium.

The children's feedback

'My one was chosen so it boosted my confidence to write more.'

'They showed us the professional way to do things and told us tips on how to write the best play.'

'I never knew how to write a play before but I do now.'

'The most rewarding part of the project was watching our play at the opening because it made me really happy and proud of our performance.'

'I enjoyed the workshop because it was really fun.'

'It gave me inspiration.'

'I thought that I wrote an excellent play script even though I didn't get mine shown.'

'I love your fantastic theatre!'

'Before the workshop, I did know how to write a play but I didn't know what exactly to add in. After the workshop I was more confident.'

Children's voices in professional performance have remarkable impact on children and can enrich the lives of artists. Quicksilver would like to bring together professionals working in this way from both the UK – especially the London groups mentioned earlier – and abroad – Barrel of Monkeys and Striking Vikings from the US to name two – to celebrate, explore, share good practice and develop this work further.

Please get in touch if you are interested in this: careyenglish@quicksilvertheatre.org

How commercial theatre supports learning in schools and the community

Creative Learning in the ATG

Julia Potts and John Coventon

The Creative Learning Regional Policy of the Ambassador Theatre Group was written in August 2009 by Julia Potts, Head of Creative Learning for the group. It is the accumulation of her twelve years' experience, working first at the Churchill Theatre, Bromley and latterly as the group's lead on Creative Learning, based in the West End. It sets out to

- facilitate access to its facilities and its performances to the widest community thereby generating and nurturing an interest in the theatre and performing arts
- enable enjoyment, develop appreciation, and facilitate participation in the performing arts with and for all members of the community
- offer opportunities to explore the pathways of creation, direction and performance, thus extending and furthering the experiences of its audiences
- offer the venues as a learning resource to ATG's communities
- help remove physical, social, economic and cultural barriers to attendance and participation

These aims will be pursued through the creation and delivery of Creative Learning programmes which:

- engage the local community in the full programme of work presented at the venue, including theatre, music, comedy and dance, through a series of events and activities which increase access to, and enjoyment of the work
- offer appropriate and high quality participatory opportunities in the performing arts for the community, by which we mean people of all ages and regardless of disability, social and economic background or cultural/ethnic background, and which complement existing activity in the region
- develop appropriate partnership projects with schools, other agencies and key community groups to use arts education as a tool in tackling a range of social agendas and local priorities

This chapter is an account of how the ATG has taken on and developed some of the active participatory programmes which were once provided by local authority specialist arts teams. It describes the current range of work ATG's Creative Learning team provides, considers longer term development targets and explores some of the ways it interacts with local schools, community groups and commercial audiences.

Founded in 1992, the Ambassador Theatre Group now owns or manages 39 theatres nationwide, making it the largest theatre group in the UK. Twelve of these venues are in London: The Apollo Victoria; Comedy; Donmar Warehouse; Duke of York's; Fortune; Lyceum; Phoenix; Piccadilly; Playhouse; Savoy; and Trafalgar Studios 1 and 2. In Greater London theatres in Bromley, Wimbledon and Richmond are also part of the group. The recent acquisition of the Live Nation chain of venues has increased ATG's regional spread.

ATG runs both regional and national tours and has recently taken some productions to Australia and to Broadway. Although ATG gets no core funding from government, it has run the business successfully enough for its recent growth to attract investment from private equity companies and investment banks.

Julia Potts began work as education officer for the Theatre of Comedy in 1998, based at the Churchill Theatre in Bromley, which 'thought it needed an education officer'. The role sat within the marketing department and was seen purely in the context of audience development. When the Ambassador Group took over the lease on the Churchill in 2000, they retained her to continue the development of work with local schools and community groups. By 2002 Julia felt she had achieved as much she could in that role and was looking to move on. But ATG recognised the value of her work and realised it was time for a strategic education plan to cover all its venues. So they created the post of Group Education Manager. ATG policy is to try to keep the employees they value so Julia was appointed to the post, combining her Group role with the original one in Bromley. By 2008 the Ambassador Theatre Group Education team was producing a much bigger, broader programme of work at its venues than in 1998 and the decision was taken to change the name from Education to the more inclusive Creative Learning.

Most of the local authorities governing ATG regional venues stipulate in their lease that there be some community participation by the theatre. This does not necessarily originate from drama teachers and schools, but may be requested by councillors or reflect a long standing commitment by the council to education in and through the arts. As ATG began taking on more theatres it realised it could make a virtue out of necessity; by offering community arts education it was ahead of its competitors. Creative Learning was seen as a highly effective tool in developing a meaningful relationship with the communities in which the theatres were based. Thus it made economic sense to maintain a community element in the venues ATG took on as it grew. Now there are fourteen permanent staff based across the regional venues in addition to Julia. There are no Creative Learning Managers covering the West End, but that is to do with the nature of the audiences and the theatre community there, of which more later.

The change from 'Education' to 'Creative Learning' in 2008 was made in recognition of the common perception that education is only about schools, whereas local needs encompass far more, although the work with schools is still important. An Ambassador Creative Learning Manager is dealing with a diverse range of projects. As Julia says, 'Outreach is a very important part of what we do. We do try to reach and work specifically with people who don't think the theatre is for them.'

Bromley Churchill Theatre

There are or have been partnership projects with Age Exchange; *Bromley in Love*, a cross generational women's project; National Theatre Connections and regular workshops with the local youth service.

In 2009 the Churchill's Youth Theatre group was selected from the 200 other youth theatre entries to perform the final play in the NT Connections Festival at the Olivier Theatre.

Outreach work includes work at the Hawthorne Centre with three English for Speakers of Other Languages (ESOL) groups and the Plaster Cast Master Class with the Princess Royal University Hospital children's ward.

The participatory programme includes regular drama classes with over 80 members, Naughty Toes Dance Classes for every age group and ability range, show related workshops and a summer school for over 100 young people.

Glasgow Theatre Royal and King's Theatre

An expanding geographical reach for the work now extends to rural communities within Argyll and Bute. In-school projects have involved working with 1500 children and young people while a further 800 have participated in production based activities.

Joint work with the Dance Consortium offers young people the chance to work with professional dancers and the community festival Go Dance 09 involved 1000 performers.

Among several partnership schemes with other venues, and supported by the Scottish Arts Council, is the establishment of a Street Team of young people tasked with using their social networking sites to promote performances and events.

The two theatres are currently working with a £270,000 grant from the Scottish Arts Council Inspire Fund on a 'boys in dance' project, developing a performance choreographed by Matthew Bourne which will tour the region.

As with most other Ambassador Creative Learning teams, Glasgow runs participatory workshops related to shows and an annual summer school.

Milton Keynes Theatre

'Progress – Success – Recognition.' This is how the Creative Learning team at Milton Keynes Theatre describe their achievements. Recognised by the local Chamber of Commerce and shortlisted for an Excellence Award in 2008, they have improved theatre access, worked with the council on anti-bullying campaigns and run a summer street dance project for 12-19 year olds.

The Creative Learning Department also became involved as Zone Advisers to the MK4U voluntary festival in which young people plan and deliver all aspects of the event, which includes rap, martial arts, free jazz, singing, various international dance forms and poetry. This attracts an audience of over 4000.

These three examples illustrate some of the work produced by ATG Creative Learning nationally. While each theatre team is responsible for its own programme, its choice and use of sessional arts workers adhere to three general principles, based on the knowledge that arts opportunities will not be taken up by communities if imposed from above:

- Creative Learning must offer some opportunities in relation to the show on the main stage
- there must be participatory work for the community, covering all ages and backgrounds generally in writing, dance and acting
- special projects will be promoted often in response to requests from partners and user groups. Many of these will originate from schools or the local authority but others come from those already involved with the theatre, for example the Somali Women's Group in Penge at the Churchill

Julia is concerned about the perception that the ATG Creative Learning team is as large as those of the National Theatre or the Royal Shakespeare Company. ATG only has the team of fourteen across the UK, supplemented by a large number of freelance practitioners, so to be effective they have to work differently to the education departments of the subsidised theatres. Community needs for Creative Learning vary from town to town and each CL manager builds her own list of arts workers to call on to serve local needs. On the positive side, Julia says, 'we have much greater freedom [than the subsidised sector] and as long as we are handling that responsibly where we are, checking and monitoring each other, I am really glad that we don't have to do Arts Council monitoring on many things.'

Every ATG Creative Learning manager has to be entrepreneurial. Commercial companies have always found it difficult to get funding even for their non-profit making work, as many Trusts and Foundations will not accept applications from commercial organisations, but there is change. When Julia first approached the Arts Council in 1998 to try to develop a relationship, she was laughed at for daring to. Now Arts Council England realise that if they are not working with the Churchill Theatre then they will have little opportunity to work in Bromley. In 2008, they granted the Churchill £77,000 for a new writing project and one of the resulting plays succeeded in a run at the Soho Theatre in the West End.

The content and purpose of the schools work has changed and developed too. In the early years, requests mostly came in for workshops on set texts at GCSE and A level, on Brecht and Artaud. The clientele were English and drama teachers. This happens much less now; they are as likely to be dealing directly with learners who wish to come in on their own terms and teachers who will be looking for anti-bullying or safeguarding programmes.

The ethos of the ATG theatres has become more child friendly. The buildings used to be closed to people, literally and metaphorically. Julia was once called urgently from her office and told, 'Julia, there is a child in the foyer!' Happily, the culture has changed dramatically and, as a matter of policy, ATG theatres are child and family-friendly.

Rehearsing on an Ambassador's stage

Schools and partnerships request assistance with the new diploma and BTEC courses. Greater emphasis on vocational courses has required ATG to create workshops on them in the Creative Learning Autumn programmes nationally. There is some concern that the new curriculum demands children learn technical theatre skills at twelve and thirteen years old when they would be better equipped to work on these aspects of theatre craft at sixteen. On the other hand, this gives good reason for opening up the theatres to young people more informally.

Requests for work experience placements have accelerated so greatly that it has become impossible for the theatres to cope with the demand and offer the standard type of placement. In consequence, CL now run carefully planned and funded Work Experience weeks which give the pupils hands on experience often denied in traditional work experience. Careers advisors should note that there is a national shortage of qualified theatre technicians.

Clearly, more and more young people are attending ATG drama classes because they want to be famous. They see performing as a way of becoming a celebrity, not as a career choice. This may be a reflection of the society we live in – they do not seem to understand that certain skills are required to succeed. Acting schools are reporting that young people cannot speak verse effectively, requiring tutors to spend time rectifying their lack of textual skill and understanding. But some argue that the skills young people have lost in verse speaking are compensated for by their more advanced movement and physical abilities.

In the last decade it has become increasingly difficult for teachers to bring young people to the theatre at all. Despite the huge pressure on teachers, and the massive increase in bureaucracy surrounding the organisation of every theatre visit, witnessing the students' excitement in seeing shows like *Woman in Black* and *Blood Brothers* make the effort worthwhile.

Many schools have a working relationship with their local Ambassadors Theatre. In the West End, the situation is more complex. Going to a West End show has always been a big night out. Experience has shown that the audiences are less tolerant of others' behaviour and may resent having students in the audience. Both actors and teachers have to prepare for young people to be in a theatre audience. Many pupils may never have been to the formal event West End theatre can be and need to know how to behave in advance as they do not want to feel unwelcome or out of place. A little preparation for a theatre visit can improve the experience for everyone.

ATG does not have a separate Creative Learning Manager for its West End theatres, but Julia hopes to rectify this soon. Having someone in post will make it easier to run workshops that introduce or reflect on the experience of some of the shows available in the ATG portfolio of London theatres. What ATG currently offer are well prepared 90 minute workshops in advance of visiting a show. A small group of advisers, including Malcolm Jones, formerly of the Theatre Museum, oversee the quality of the teachers' workshops. The current workshop on *Legally Blonde* is particularly popular and successful. In the regions the venues also have teacher groups who advise and support the CL teams.

It is a two way process. ATG directors need to know what texts are appearing in the Drama, Theatre Studies and English curriculum at A level and GCSE and the teacher groups can keep them informed.

The West End sets different challenges. The development of the teachers' workshop for the recent ATG production of an Arthur Miller play began with Julia asking the producer to provide a suitable programme of study. While there was support for the idea in principle, the problem was, as always, Creative Learning had no resources to fund the workshops, although it could have provided the freelance theatre worker to run them. The producer might think workshops would be worthwhile but funding them adds significant cost to the production budget. It is often forgotten that with single shows brought in by ATG, it is the producers who have to recover their costs and provide a return to the production's investors. It is a circle that is hard to square.

In August 2010, Richard Pulford, Chief Executive of the Society of London Theatre (SOLT), told us:

> The formulation we normally use is that historically, out of every ten shows produced commercially in the West End, on average one will make a profit, two will break even and seven will make some loss. Having said that, we normally add that some profitable shows provide very good returns indeed.

> Although we don't have precise figures, my sense is that the number of shows making a profit has increased somewhat in the last few years.

So cheaper tickets for students and schools are not a priority, and schools work and reduced prices often become available only when a show is not selling its full price tickets well. But by then it may be too late for that production to continue. Julia defends independent commercial producers in their apparent reluctance to support schools programmes. She says it is not that they do not value the idea, it is just that they have other priorities. There is no public money in most commercial productions, so it is hard to make the case for public benefit.

Over the past decade the role of Group Education Manager and latterly Head of Creative Learning has become more connected to the centre of ATG. There is a genuine commitment to the work from the board of directors and the CEO. Creative Learning costs relatively little in terms of the whole business, yet it has been a challenge to maintain the work's integrity and core values in the face of commercial pressures. Julia feels that the embedding of Creative Learning within the organisation is an important achievement and hopes it will remain so. But the future for ATG, as for many arts organisations, is increasingly uncertain.

Julia is looking to the medium and longer term view and wishes to see a Creative Learning Centre in every regional centre, with more collaborative work across ATG venues.

> While the work is centralised and embedded, it is still difficult to do it in a commercial setting – you constantly have to be an advocate for the work. This has a healthy side in that it does make you very good at fighting your corner. We have all these buildings that used to be closed to people, literally and metaphorically, and my job is, 'how do we open them up?'

Brand recognition – as ATG rather than the Churchill Theatre – will help this process. Thanks to the success of the company, there is greater need than ever to produce really good shows to go into such a large number of venues. Everything is on the up.

And for the future, she says:

> Clearly it is going to be tough for the next few years, as it will be for the arts in general. But I think what I do and what my colleagues do has become a core part of what theatres do, and if we are doing this work well, we are helping ourselves survive as well. We are making ourselves more sustainable by creating ownership and support for theatre with a wider range of people and audiences. I see lots of theatres, including ours, producing very good work and lots of people who still care very much that the local theatre is thriving. We will have to be very clever, nimble and alert to opportunity over the coming months, but it is a challenge I think we can meet.

The professional organisation for teachers and others, past, present and future

About London Drama

Chris Lawrence

Early Days: Local Education Authority Support

L ondon Drama is the professional association for teachers of drama in London. Our strap line is, 'we are run by teachers for teachers across the capital and beyond,' and this sums up the continuing voluntary nature of the organisation, its strategic ambitions and outlook since it began in 1955 when it was called the London Schools Drama Association (LSDA). In those days everyone knew London Drama and every school received the *Drama Bulletin, Broadsheet* and later *London Drama* magazine, all funded and published by the Inner London Education Authority (ILEA).

With the abolition of ILEA by the Thatcher government in 1990, *London Drama* magazine and London Drama itself suddenly became vulnerable. However, both were so valued and respected that neither was permitted to be destroyed. London Drama was constituted as a limited company and a charity with a voluntary membership base and the organising committee became official trustees of the charity. *London Drama* magazine was adopted by the newly formed National Drama, renamed *The Drama Magazine* and later simply *Drama*, thus maintaining an unbroken tradition from 1955 to the present day through both organisations in two different ways. London Drama has continued its support for *Drama* magazine, buying it in for its members, and serving on its editorial Team.

Going it Alone: Principles of Survival

The problem: fragmentation and isolation

One of the most serious consequences of the demise of the ILEA has been the fragmentation and isolation of each borough and, through the policy of Local Management of Schools (LMS), of each individual school within each borough. Faced with these unpromising circumstances, an inevitable result of the political theory that 'there is no such thing as Society', the role thrust upon London Drama is contradicting this fragmentation at strategic level by providing a sense of community and integration of drama resources across the whole capital in the spirit of the tradition of drama provision in London since 1955 – but without financial or human resources. A tall order but, as they say, 'you can't kill the spirit!' and the proof is that London Drama has survived for twenty years by going it alone. How has it done so? Are there key principles for London Drama's survival?

The drama movement

If you are no longer supported by a strategic infrastructure or by an official funding body then you need to build and maintain strong grassroots support amongst those who have an interest in your survival, in London Drama's case drama teachers and theatre practitioners. These are the people who invest in London Drama by paying a membership fee which, when all are put together, lend London Drama an independence and stability – for as long as the membership maintains confidence in the organisation. Communication with and support of its grassroots membership is a key to sustaining what is best described as a *movement* – a living ongoing community of drama teachers in and around London. It is vital that this movement is nurtured and supported – and inspired. London Drama's programme of day and twilight courses in drama is at the heart of that endeavour.

An all year round programme

London Drama maintains a Continuing Professional Development (CPD) programme of day courses and evening courses all year round because, in our view, drama teachers require CPD support as and when they need it and on an ongoing basis. It also enables us to respond to needs flexibly and promptly, as in the case of the place of drama in the New Primary Curriculum. Our courses are in two strands: day courses, usually held on Saturdays to avoid problems of cover and release, could be described as being for inspiration, challenge and refreshment; while our evening course strand tends to focus more on curriculum demands and classroom support. While we actively en-courage our long standing members to share their experience and wisdom via the latter programme we have also formed excellent relationships through the day courses with many of the writers featured in this book and with theatre companies like Complicité, Shared Experience, Frantic Assembly, DV8 and Improbable.

The office

That the association has an office is not only a distinguishing feature of London Drama, it is also a key component of its survival. It is a tangible manifestation of the movement it serves and represents: maintaining the office is symbolic of maintaining the movement. And it indicates that there is a need to take seriously the administration of a programme like the one described. London Drama has made a point of maintaining an office in the London Borough of Camden; originally at the ILEA Drama and Tape Centre (later renamed the Holborn Centre for Performing Arts), then at the Central School of Speech and Drama until their new building work began in 2003/4; and now with the Diorama of which London Drama is an Associate. We are temporarily based at The Crypt Centre in Munster Square while the Diorama (opposite Great Portland Street station) is being redeveloped to include, in phase one, The New Diorama Theatre, the new home of Quicksilver Theatre Company and, in phase two, workshops, rehearsal spaces and offices, one of which will be our brand new and – hopefully – final home.

Office holders

Remarkably, London Drama has had only two office holders (administrators) since 1955: Win Bayliss, and me. Win's stewardship of London Drama spanned an incredible 48 years from 1955 with the formation of the LSDA until 2003, when she reluctantly retired at the age of 89. My own administration has run from 1995 to the present. Consistency on this scale develops in any small organisation a remarkable rootedness, resilience and focus; perhaps unfashionable qualities in this throw away age but rare and vital equipment for survival.

Publications

While London Drama has been unable financially to maintain its own magazine or other publications like *Drama Guidelines* and *Drama Strategies*, written by London drama teachers, it has consistently managed to maintain a drama newsletter, now called Dialogue. Dialogue is usually four pages, produced six times a year with news, reviews, reflections on practice and theatre listings. By also buying in *Drama* magazine the tradition of encouraging teachers to write about and share their work is maintained as an aspect of best practice and contact with the membership takes a practical form – they receive something tangible.

The Book Service

The London Drama Book Service, originally built up and maintained by Win Bayliss, is nowadays in competition with Amazon so times are a bit hard. But what Amazon does not do is provide bookstalls at Drama conferences, a tradition begun by Win and still a distinguishing feature of London Drama's practice. It is one thing to browse books online; it is quite another to see a full range laid out before you with the option of looking inside the pages. So many drama books are available now that building a small drama library is a practical possibility and can be especially useful in primary schools, providing a non-threatening introduction to drama for a tentative colleague and a clear signal that drama is valued and supported.

Current Achievements: Working at a Strategic Level

Despite the difficulties of going it alone we have recently seen some significant successes, both London wide and in local areas.

London Drama and the colleges

We have a good relationship with the London colleges who run courses in drama. When we were based at the Central School of Speech and Drama, we made good friends with staff and our evening course programme is largely based there still. London Drama is now a sponsor of the Centre for Arts and Learning at Goldsmiths College, and contributes to the PGCE student programme and interview process. Goldsmiths also hosts a Research and Study Unit in Drama Education generated from material from London Drama's archive; Central School hosts a twin Study unit in Theatre Education materials. Links to these are available on the Resources section of our website. Middlesex University and the Institute of Education also support London Drama, for instance, through the Students Welcome event.

London Drama Students Welcome

The London Drama Students Welcome has grown over the years into a significant event in the calendars of the PGCE Drama courses in the London universities and latterly also of Reading University. Usually held at the Institute of Education on a Saturday in Autumn at the start of the PGCE students' courses, it represents the first steps towards building and maintaining a community of drama teachers from the very beginning. As well as a friendly welcome to London, it offers an introduction to London Drama as the students' professional association. Workshops are led by the tutors of the PGCE Drama courses, backed up by the ubiquitous London Drama bookstall. Usually around fifty students attend and last year Middlesex and Goldsmiths

Universities subsidised student membership of London Drama and Middlesex subsidised the course fees for its attending students.

STEP

Many of the plays of Shakespeare, Ben Jonson and others were first performed in theatres built in London's oldest borough, Southwark. As if continuing an ancient tradition, many theatre companies, large and small are based in Southwark, including Shakespeare's Globe, London Bubble, The Unicorn Theatre, Theatre Peckham, The Union Theatre, Southwark Playhouse, the Blue Elephant Theatre and many small theatre companies.

STEP stands for Southwark Theatres Education Partnership. This was founded in 2003 following a discussion that I, on behalf of Southwark Arts Forum and London Drama, had with Simon Hughes, MP for North Southwark and Bermondsey, about the massive contradiction that existed in Southwark between the richness and historical significance of theatre provision in the borough and the comparative poverty of the education sector, then suffering the indignity of being in special measures. Would it not be a good idea to get the two worlds into greater dialogue? From this the Southwark Theatres Education Partnership was born, to create an organisation dedicated to facilitating partnerships between theatres and educational institutions in the borough.

From this small beginning STEP had the momentum and imaginative impact of an idea whose time had come: with the added influence of a local MP's support, theatre companies got involved, committed themselves to many meetings, appointed a festival director. At the first STEP Festival Sir Ian McKellen was guest of honour at the opening ceremony at Shakespeare's Globe. When he arrived the performing children cried, 'it's Gandalf!' It was a thrill to hear Sir Ian give his distinguished wholehearted backing to the plan but also the leader of Southwark Council pledging support to encourage more drama and theatre in Southwark schools. We knew then that STEP was truly born: it had caught the imagination of the council itself.

Since this heady time STEP has developed an annual Festival of Theatre and Drama events and practical workshops, including one on theatre review writing led by Michael Billington, and teachers' In-Service Education and Training (INSET) led by London Drama. There is also a year round programme developing a drama and theatre emphasis in the new Creative and Media Diploma, facilitating partnerships between schools and theatres. What is happening in Southwark is a fine model of how the *zeitgeist* of a borough or local authority can be transformed from an alien and obstructive environ-ment for the arts to a highly supportive environment for drama and theatre. London Drama, along with Southwark theatres and drama practitioners, is at the heart of it. STEP is now a charity and as a trustee I try to ensure that London Drama continues to have a voice at this key strategic level (see the website at www.step-partnership.co.uk).

Southwark Primary Drama Champions

The phase of education hardest hit creatively by the demise of the ILEA's re-sourcing of the arts and the relentless waves of political initiatives is the primary sector. But the momentum generated by the success of STEP made it easier to take another step forward to build a supportive infrastructure for teaching drama in primary schools in the borough.

One of the original financial investors in STEP, the *Financial Times*, also based in Southwark, was approached in 2006 to fund a special project: to develop a cohort of twenty primary school teachers who would champion drama in their own and neighbouring schools. The idea caught their imagination: FT staff had been supporting listening to children read in primary schools but this proposal was altogether more ambitious and entrepreneurial and this appealed to them. It was before the recession. They asked how much we needed – £20,000 – and wrote the cheque. Southwark Drama Champions was born. London Drama – as well as STEP – was involved at the inception in partnership with the Literacy and Drama Consultant for Southwark, Nina Birch, and the Arts Officer for Southwark, Coral Flood. The initial session was held over two consecutive days with practitioners from Shakespeare's Globe leading sessions on movement and approaches to Shakespeare while Pam Bowell of National Drama and Jonothan Neelands of Warwick University led sessions on process drama.

The Southwark Drama Champions action based research project is now three years old and organises regular drama CPD events, each with a different focus with London Drama involved in the administration and evaluation. Future plans include accreditation of the programme by South Bank University as part of a masters degree in Drama.

Primary Drama developments in Croydon

One of the most exciting areas of development for drama in the primary sector has been the recent partnership with the London Borough of Croydon. Here it is not the story of the long march as in Southwark: it happened much more suddenly, almost by accident.

Last year David Wilcox, a primary headteacher in Croydon, found London Drama's website via Google and asked whether we ran drama courses for primary teachers, as he could find nothing available. We assured him he had come to the right place. What has developed since is the much prized – and rare – partnership at borough level via the Assistant Head of Croydon Music and Arts, Helen Bretherick, her literacy team colleagues and David Wilcox. A programme has been arranged to develop a drama network for primary teachers funded by the literacy team in partnership with London Drama. Twenty seven keen teachers attended the initial half day event and returned for a further day event in the summer term. Once the Croydon Primary Drama Network is established, London Drama should be able to provide on-going support and inspiration.

With the Southwark and Croydon models up and running, London Drama is determined to set about the long job of creating thriving drama networks for primary teachers in many more London boroughs.

The Future: London Drama and the Digital Age
Is there a future for professional associations?
The socio-political context is so hostile to child centred learning and by implication to drama in schools that it might be thought that there is no future for a professional association dedicated to these ideals. But I believe the opposite is the case: it is precisely because theatre and drama in education is under threat and the official curriculum is so arid and prescriptive that an organisation like London Drama is so necessary to provide inspiration and encouragement to fellow professionals to keep the spirit of true education alive. London Drama sees itself as a rallying point and an independent voice – albeit often in the wilderness – for the stewardship of drama in educational settings at a time when the political climate has got colder and training in the discipline has been steadily eroded and watered down. In short, London Drama represents the real deal, and has also embraced the technology that will support it in its survival.

Our website
London Drama's new website at www.londondrama.org is based on an e-commerce framework, offering a series of products for membership, courses and books, and a shopping basket. However, the e-commerce aspect is only half the story: the other is the growing networks we are fostering, for example, the Secondary Forum group and the Drama Champions web pages plus theatre companies, freelance drama practitioners and borough organisers,

who have their own directory page which they manage themselves. Nearly every aspect of what the association is and does is there for all to see.

London Drama E-News

Supplementing the website and *Dialogue,* the London Drama E-News keeps in touch with members regularly with news, opportunities and reminders about what London Drama events are currently available.

Email groups, online surveys and evaluations

The Google email group is an ideal facility for community building and contacting members with a particular interest, e.g. all secondary members, via email. Google's online response form linked to an online spreadsheet automatically enables us to conduct surveys and to replace paper based evaluations for our courses with online evaluations. Responses can be shared online with the committee as they come in so we keep track of our members' needs and fulfilments.

We also have an Intranet website for sharing important administrative information amongst committee members and arranging their availability for meetings.

Conclusion

London Drama is not only steeped in history as the two Research and Study Units held at Goldsmiths and Central School testify. It is also fully embracing the communication media of the future. This is essential for a small organisation with an ambition to work at a strategic level, building or rebuilding infrastructures for drama to thrive.

Its successes, its focus on PGCE students, its work in Southwark and Croydon, are remarkable models of good practice. But it is constantly aware that, in a city as big as London, with general lack of support for drama at borough level and huge public sector cuts looming, there is still a long way to go. It will take determination and a capacity for survival – fortunately, qualities which London Drama is not short of.

the last word

Parties recognise the right of the child to rest and leisure, to engage in play and recreational activities appropriate to the age of the child and to participate freely in cultural life and the arts.

Parties shall respect and promote the right of the child to participate fully in cultural and artistic life and shall encourage the provision of appropriate and equal opportunities for cultural, artistic, recreational and leisure activities.

Article 31
The United Nations Convention of the Rights of the Child
1989